ON THE PUBLIC FACE OF ARCHITECTURE

ON THE PUBLIC FACE OF ARCHITECTURE

THE WINTER CONVERSAZIONE FOR 1990

SALLYANNE ATKINSON, NATHAN GLAZER,
HANS HALLEN, NORMAN HAMMOND,
DARYL JACKSON, RICHARD MACCORMAC, ROGER SCRUTON,
HARRY SEIDLER, DELL UPTON.

ROBERT W. GASTON, EDITOR

The Boston, Melbourne, Oxford Conversazioni on Culture and Society

ISBN 0 646 07053 3

Design: The Greenwood Design Group
Film Production and Printing: Southbank Communications Group

Foreword

None of these papers requires preamble or introduction; they all speak eloquently for themselves; but the occasion itself does need some explanation. The Boston, Melbourne, Oxford *Conversazioni* on Culture and Society is a tripartite arrangement between Boston University, La Trobe University, in Melbourne, and Wadham College, Oxford, *to combine resources in order to address the great themes of our time in a cross disciplinary manner* and with the participation of persons from outside the academic ambit, whose experience and knowledge my colleagues and I consider to be illuminating and essential for the success of this intellectual enterprise.

The Public Face of Architecture is the title of a book edited by Nathan Glazer and Mark Lilla, respectively a sociologist and a political scientist. Having been adopted as the theme for *The Winter Conversazione for 1990*, it was then considered from the vantage point of the Chairman of a Department of Anthropology; a Professor of Philosophy; the then Lord Mayor of Brisbane; a Professor of Sociology; a Professor of Architectural History and four architects.

This *Winter Conversazione* has derived some gentle inspiration from John Ruskin's *The Stones of Venice*, in which the renowned man of arts and letters suggested that while many people may go through life untouched by painting, ignorant of poetry and indifferent to music, no one living in a civilised society can remain unaffected by architecture. This is the most public of the arts and the one that most faithfully reflects the nature and disposition of the society that sustains it. Moreover, Ruskin was convinced that "Things... are noble or ignoble in proportion to the fullness of life which either they themselves enjoy, or of whose action they bear the evidence." In other words, the creature bears the mark of the creator. This applies to all the cultural artifacts made by human hands, but especially to architecture, the most public of all the arts, and the one that is tellingly and inextricably bound up with life in society. The architecture of a people, thought Ruskin, is the mirror of their genesis and moral condition. This is the main theme of *The Stones of Venice*, in which he proposes that the architecture of the sea-city reflects its rise, the splendour of its golden age, and its eventual dissipation and moral decrepitude.

The order in which the papers were presented at the *Conversazione* was in part influenced by this intriguing thesis; thus, after two introductory papers by Professor Nathan Glazer and Alderman Sallyanne Atkinson, the rest were arranged under three headings; "The Stones of the Old World" (including the papers by Professor Roger Scruton and Mr Richard MacCormack); "The Stones of the New World" (including the papers by Professors Norman Hammond and Dell Upton; and "The Stones of Our World" (including the papers by Mr. Harry Seidler, Mr. Daryl Jackson and Mr. Hans Hallen).

Responding to the elegant exigencies of the subject under discussion, it was decided not to hold all meetings in the same place, traditionally the Council Room of Glenn College, La Trobe University, but to seek other architecturally appropriate ambits within which to consider the wider implications of our subject. In keeping with tradition, the inaugural session was held at Glenn College; "The Stones of the Old World" met in the Committee Room of the Legislative Council, in Parliament House; " The Stones of the New World", in Trinity College Chapel, The University of Melbourne; "The Stones of Our World" in Shell House, in Spring Street.

This *Conversazione*, like all those that came before it and, we hope, all the ones that will follow, did not lead to the passing of resolutions, declarations of intent, or motions approved by acclamation. In the words of Michael Oakeshott, quoted elsewhere in this publication, this conversation "has no predetermined course, we do not ask what it is 'for', and we do not judge its excellence by its conclusion; it has no conclusion, but is always put by for another day. Its integration is not superimposed but springs from the quality of the voices which speak, and its value lies in the relics it leaves behind in the mind of those who participate..." On this occasion, we hope that the publication of these papers, made possible by a most generous grant by the Shell Company of Australia Limited, will extend the circle of those who may derive information, inspiration, perhaps even enlightenment from our diffident incursion into one of the great themes of our time.

Claudio Véliz
University Professor and Professor of History. Director, The University Professors, Boston University.

CONTENTS

BUILDING FOR THE PUBLIC: WHAT HAS GONE WRONG?

Nathan Glazer

This *Conversazione* is an exercise in the mixture of realms and specialities. Nevertheless, a sociologist speaking of architecture and public building feels the need for some kind of preliminary justification for dealing with the subject. The justification, briefly stated, is that building for the public implies that there is some legitimacy in the response of the public: whether it uses the building or not, whether it likes it or not, whether it feels it is an embellishment of the public life, worthy of admiration and pride, or not. There are of course practical needs a building must meet, and that play a role in all these judgements the public makes. Yet, regardless of our professional identification or our incapacity in dealing with professional aspects of architecture and design, our response to that most elusive quality of building and urban design – its aesthetic quality, do we find it beautiful or not, and do we find it suitably beautiful for the place and function for which it is designed? – cannot be ignored. It would be to act like moles to limit ourselves to only practical considerations: the city, any city, reaches for more than that, and it is with that "more" that I deal in these comments.

So I consider the range of issues that come up in the criticism of architecture, a range elegantly and satisfactorily put in the words of Sir Henry Wotton: "Well-building hath three conditions: Commodity, Firmness and Delight". Wotton was adapting Vitruvius, and I take the quotation from Geoffrey Scott's *The Architecture of Humanism*.[1] Commodity: it suits its purpose, it is a proper envelope for the activities that will take place in it. Firmness: it stands up without cracks or stains, pieces don't fall off, the parts fit together, it looks solid. And delight, the most elusive but also the most important of qualities.

John Ruskin, despite his disdain for Vitruvius, and his hatred for the Renaissance architecture that, with these introductory words of Wotton, Scott was defending, says very much the same thing: "We have three great branches of architectural virtue, and we require of any building:

1. That it act well, and do the things it was intended to do in the best way.
2. That it speak well, and say the things it was intended to say in the best words.
3. That it look well, and please us by its presence whatever it has to do or say"[2].

---

1 First published, London, 1914; New York, 1954 edition p. 16.
2 *The Stones of Venice*, 3 vols., London 1851-53; Everyman's ed., London, 1906, I, p.23.

Ruskin then acknowledges that there can be no general laws as to how buildings "speak": it would depend, as we would say, on the culture. So he too is agreeing that it is commodity and firmness – how a building acts – and delight – how it looks – that are the chief criteria by which we judge architecture.

Enough for authorities. But, you will say, there is no accounting for taste, whether in art or building. And so when we express our discontent with so much building for the public today, it is easy to be answered, "but wait fifty years: we or our descendants will then find it powerful, or effective, or interesting, or charming, and we'll want to preserve it". But I do not think that answer will serve. Something has happened, and for most of our public building, we won't be eager to preserve it, and we won't find it powerful or beautiful or interesting: we'll be sorry it's there, and we'll wonder how it got there, and how we can improve it or replace it.

We have a number of tasks here in this *Conversazione*. One is to ask whether the current widespread dissatisfaction represents only the normal ebb and flow of public taste, the kind of thing which permitted Gibbon to say in the late 18th century of the square of San Marco in Venice, that it was "decorated with the worst architecture I ever saw"[3] or that permitted John Ruskin to write, fifty years later, that Bath was a "horrible" place.[4] I will argue that our present situation represents considerably more than a shift in taste or fashion, more than what we saw in the past with the turn against the restrained classical and Georgian in the Gothic revival of the mid nineteenth century: or in the Beaux-Arts revival of the late nineteenth century that condemned the Gothic and Romanesque that was then popular. What we deal with now is not a battle of the styles, even though the argument between the Modernists and the Post-Modernists, the International style and whatever is happening to challenge it, looks like a battle of the styles. In comparison with those muscular conflicts of the past between authoritative views over how a building should look, we deal with the merest skirmishes around a common norm. And a norm that leaves most of us discontented.

The second task, more difficult, is to explore the bases of our discontent. Is it mere nostalgia? An ignorant (in the sense of uninformed about design) preference for what is common and familiar, perhaps vulgar, against what is sophisticated, refined, complex?

---

3 John Rosenberg, *The Darkening Glass*, New York, 1961, p. 48.
4 Michael Brooks, *John Ruskin and Victorian Architecture*, Rutgers, 1987, p. 6.

2

And a third task: once we explore the bases of our discontent, we will have to consider whether the conditions of modern life permit anything else. If they don't, we may have to stop there, whatever our discontent. If we think they do, we'll ask just what can be done to improve public architecture.

Our topic is somewhat ambiguous. By "the public face of architecture" we can mean all building. All our architecture is in one sense "public". Homes of the most modest scale are seen, and generally meant to be seen, and whether meant to be seen or not, form part of the urban fabric. And the public – the authorities, the laws and regulations, and our neighbours – play a very large role in how we may build our own houses. Even the buildings of secret societies present a public face to the world, and often a quite magnificent public face, as we see in the buildings of Masonic societies.

But it is our public buildings and spaces, our capitals and courthouses, our opera houses and theatres, our colleges and universities, our public squares and parks, with which we are most concerned: they all make a rather more substantial effort to impress, to shape public spaces, to declare their public function, to strengthen in those who view them a civic consciousness, a pride in government, city, public life, and major institutions.

Indeed, when it comes to private building, that is, the building of houses, there is really no great discontent over design: there is over cost, which is a different matter. The building of houses seems to follow traditional designs, for the most part. Seventy years of modernist innovation in house design has produced its masterpieces, and continues to produce its annual crop of prizewinners, but has very little influence on the houses most builders put up and most people buy and live in. Oddly, it is only when the building of houses becomes *public* building – the public housing of the United States, the council housing of Britain – that we see the characteristic grumbling against modernism and the international style emerge.

The public at large, and even the sophisticated public, is in the position of knowing what it likes and what it doesn't like, but not being able to explain just why. Controversy concentrates around the new, which one would think would best represent present tastes and present needs. It is much more muted around the old: indeed, anything old today bears a presumption that it is better than anything that might replace it.

Architects are properly annoyed and even outraged when an ever more powerful preservationism and distrust of contemporary professional architectural taste and capacity denies them sites and opportunities, and restricts many to modernizing old buildings. What has happened, they ask in irritation, to that forward-looking spirit that characterized our Western societies until recently? We would not have thought twice in the Renaissance about tearing down old buildings and even using their very stones for new ones; or in the Baroque age of transforming every Gothic church in the new mode. In the sequence of historical revivals in the nineteenth century we found every new style (presumably based on an old) better than the one before it. And we were quite ready to find the Victorian and Edwardian buildings of the last historic revivals repulsive and worthy of replacement by modern steel, concrete, and glass until just a few years ago. As a result, we now have books labelled *Lost New York* or *Lost Boston* or *Lost London*, and I am sure we will in time have *Lost Melbourne*, appealing not merely to the taste for the quaint and the archaic and the old-fashioned, but to a veritable and deeply felt sense of loss and tragedy in considering what we have destroyed.

Perhaps the strangest part of the whole story is that it was when architects and planners became most concerned with improving the lives of ordinary people, of citizens, with creating a better environment for all, that to present eyes they committed some of their most grievous errors. We do not fault much today the architects and planners who built for kings and princes, for the great powers of church and state. Indeed, our democratic societies spend fortunes to maintain those extravagant buildings, squares, parks, that were designed not for the people, for ourselves, but for the private pleasure of kings and prelates, great nobles or merchant princes. So much on the other hand that we have built explicitly for ourselves, for the ordinary people, we now find unattractive and even worthy of destruction before its time, as in the case of the public housing of the United States or the council estates of Britain. Some of these have been dynamited, after lying vandalized and half-vacant; others seem candidates for destruction. How is it possible that great quantities of housing, following the models and prescriptions of the most distinguished architects, built to high standards, should have failed so miserably?

I am not speaking of a phenomenon limited to Britain, where Prince Charles' complaints about modern building – the office buildings around and planned around St. Paul's in London, the earlier proposed modernist addition to the National Gallery, the replacement of Edwardian buildings in the city of London by a building by a major modern architect, James Stirling, – have evoked such wide response. When one looks around where one lives – whether in Cambridge and Boston, or I would assume, Melbourne, which I know is a centre of new building – we will find much that is new no improvement, and generally some falling off from what is old. I live in Cambridge, Massachusetts, and one might begin there to consider what has gone wrong. For example, consider the sequence of buildings that have been put up to house the Harvard Museums. The original Fogg Museum of Art of 1925 is no masterpiece *(fig. 1):* it is simply representative of its time and its designer lurks under the corporate name of Coolidge, Shepley, Bulfinch, and Abbott, which built much of brick Georgian revival Harvard. A second Harvard museum for the arts of Germany, built during and after World War I, evokes some South German or Austrian church. *(fig. 2)* The last in the series is by the aforementioned distinguished British architect, James Stirling. *(fig. 3)* It has virtues: its interior provides a good deal of usable space, more for its size than its predecessors. But it is not a building to make the spirit soar. And this, recall, is a museum.

Fig. 1 The Fogg Museum of Art

Fig. 2 The Busch-Reisinger Museum

Fig. 3 The Sackler Museum

Or consider the buildings in which the Sociology Department has successively made its home. Again, we begin with a characteristic building of its time, Emerson Hall *(fig. 4)* (Guy Lowell, 1900), quite similar in its red brick and limestone to the Fogg Museum. And we move to a grand new building *(fig. 5)* by the architect Minoru Yamasaki, again no unknown: he is the designer of the World Trade Center in New York City, the two towers that were for a time the tallest buildings in the world. His building reflects one of those modest twists in the history of the International style – an effort to bring back something like decoration or ornament, to decorate somewhat the bare box. It is generally disliked. It doesn't have enough elevators – as seems true of all tall academic buildings. Its plaza seems pointless – swept by strong winds in winter, broiling in summer. It relates to nothing else at Harvard. It produces wind storms around its base because it is so high.

Fig. 4 Emerson Hall

Fig. 5 William James Hall

Or consider another sequence, the buildings that have housed the School of Design and Architecture. The first, by a distinguished Beaux-Arts architect, was unfortunately torn down: it looked grand, and the people who lived and worked in it liked it, but it is true it had little usable space behind its large entry hall. A more functional building, Robinson Hall (McKim, 1904) replaced it. *(fig. 6)* It matches the brick and limestone Emerson Hall, which makes the opposite side of the square on which it sits, and is respectful to it – it is roughly the same shape and height, and of the same materials. But then a new structure was put up by the major contemporary Australian architect John Andrews, Gund Hall. It is a long expanse of concrete, with its upper section overhanging the street and supported on thin concrete columns. Its rear is a great sheet of sloping glass, covering the drafting spaces of the students, and quite striking at night. But its interior spaces seem cut up, unshaped, and left over, as they so often do

8

in contemporary buildings put up to express a single major theme. It was rebuilt at great expense only a few years after it was erected to deal with some functional problems.

Fig. 6 Robinson Hall

As you see, I am not stacking the deck on this little tour of a portion of my home grounds. Stirling, Yamasaki, and Andrews are no minor contemporary architects. One can stack it by going to the Cambridge courthouses, another sequence of buildings put up to house the same functions. The first building was put up perhaps by James Bulfinch, a well-known early nineteenth century architect of Boston and Massachusetts. It is a modest and pleasing structure, of red brick, symmetrical with a tower, suited to the small town Cambridge then was. The second is a rather grander structure, late nineteenth century, with giant red brick columns. The third, a building of the seventies, is simply a horror. It is of varied materials, tall, with no sense of dignity or grandeur. Its only virtue must be that its mean and low and hardly visible entry fulfils Federal requirements for access by the handicapped.

If I went across the river to Boston, the contrasts between the grand Boston Public Library of McKim, Mead and White, and its new addition by Philip Johnson; or the old stone City Hall and its replacement in concrete by Kallman and McKinnell would make the same points.

Some of the things for which contemporary architects are criticised emerge from these contrasts. Thus, they don't relate themselves to what has gone before. When they claim they do, ordinary folk don't see the relationship. The architects of Emerson Hall, Robinson Hall, and the Fogg Museum, created a square with their buildings. Each successive building related to the first building put up in this area, by a truly distinguished American architect working in the 1870s, H.H. Richardson. Even though we deal with a stretch of fifty years during which the four buildings around this square were erected, each successor architect to Richardson seemed to make some acknowledgment – in the use of a common material, brick, or a common height, or siting the building so that it took into account the fact that other buildings were there – to what had gone before. The Cambridge courthouses – until the monstrosity of the newest – also related to each other, and this over a longer period of a hundred years. They too were all in brick, and even if of different scale, in their siting acknowledged another building was there. Which is why a pleasant little park or square can now be placed between the two earlier courthouses. Nothing of any charm or interest will ever be placed around the new Courthouse.

A second problem of our newer buildings emerges from this little tour: scale. New replacements are generally larger, much larger, than the older buildings, and scale presents difficulties. It is true more students must be housed, more faculty, more research facilities, more judges, courts and trials. The old buildings simply will not do because they are too small, and we would not want really – unless we are truly utopian – to cut down on the size of our universities and colleges, to restrict the number of our students, to limit access to the courts, or to reduce the size of our jails. All this is a product both of the increase of our populations – which may be seen as either desirable or unfortunate, but is a given fact – and the greater access of more people today to the goods of society – its colleges and universities, its courts and public services, its libraries and its museums. So all these institutions expand, and build on a scale that creates difficulties.

Huge buildings we admire were put up in the past, too. So there are other things besides scale that are problematic. One of them – which we will come to shortly – is that the features which used to structure scale for the eye, manage scale, – systems of ornament and decoration – are no longer available to contemporary architects. So we are confronted by the huge height of buildings of repeated floors, the extended expanse of boring walls.

Scale is a problem. The most admired composition of buildings and spaces in the United States is the University of Virginia by Thomas Jefferson. Our third president was also a great architect and designer. He had many virtues. No one disputes the elegance and beauty of Jefferson's "academical village", with its two rows of modest structures, facing each other across a beautiful lawn, with one end closed by an exquisite domed building, the Rotunda, originally designed for a library. But no library of any size could now be fitted into it, or into many other domed buildings once put up for libraries, whether the Radcliffe Camera at Oxford, the British Museum, our own Library of Congress, or your own State Library of Victoria. "Why must it be so big?", asked Prince Charles when he was shown the main office building of Canary Wharf. Alas, it can't be helped. Things must be bigger. Bigger may mean a greater opportunity for more grandeur and impact, a truly powerful statement of what it is the building is trying to symbolise – government, learning, culture. But combined with other contemporary features, it sets the architect a problem he finds it hard to meet.

Scale means that the attention to detail that characterises all great architecture must simply go by the board. The work is disaggregated and parcelled out to many designers. In addition, of course, the contemporary large building must in some degree be shaped by practical needs, determined by structural engineers, air conditioning and heating engineers, experts in electrical and electronic and communications facilities, etc. The architect is limited to the big picture in broad outline. When one considers, in the history of architecture, the degree of attention given by great figures in the past to the single facade of a church – the type of column, the decoration of a window, the placement and size of doorways –and when one reads how the details of these facades were disputed over decades and centuries, one realizes that modern building is a very different thing.

There are some architects today who believe, as Ruskin did, that they should be craftsmen and builders of their work as well as architects, and involved in every detail of their designs. The most distinguished is the theorist Christopher Alexander. But the architect who believes he must pay attention to every detail, or even more, work with his own hands on his designs, must expect to live on his earnings as a teacher and writer and foundation grantee, rather than as an architect. As one contemporary admirer of Ruskin writes, "It is easy to understand why the entrepreneur-architects of Ruskin's day regarded him as 'a malevolent of the worst description'. His visual criteria, if taken to heart, would have reduced them to spending a lifetime on two, perhaps three buildings; and while such a proceeding might have resulted in architecture comparable in aesthetic qualities with the medieval and early Renaissance buildings which had trained Ruskin's eye and established his tastes, the results, in terms of the architects' incomes, would have been disastrous".[5]

One of those other contemporary features also evident in our tour is the range of new materials the architect must choose from. All the early buildings I have shown offered the architect few alternatives in terms of material to build with. It was brick or stone or wood. And if it was to be brick or stone or wood the building wall naturally broke down into small units: courses of brick or stone, wooden siding or shingles, all a help in moderating large scale. The unbroken expanses of concrete of William James Hall and Gund Hall were not available, and the glass and steel so typical in contemporary large buildings were not available. The materials for building were given by the site and place, with few alternatives: in Cambridge it was generally brick – it was even used for sidewalks – in other places it might be local stone, or wood. Can we deny ourselves the opportunities offered by new materials? I think not. If we were limited to hand-laid brick or cut stone, it would be impossible to build on the scale we need. Individually, we can withdraw. We can build new colleges on the scale of Jefferson's University of Virginia, for 300 students and 20 faculty. But that won't answer the needs of the many thousands who clamour for entry.

We cannot imagine society adopting a self-denying ordinance and rejecting access to steel and glass and concrete and whatever variants of these or other building materials are now available. This may mean that the buildings leak, or the windows pop out, or the concrete is marred by ugly rain stains, or that we find it harder than we expected to heat and cool the building – and all these things are true, because no new building material has undergone the long testing period of stone, brick, and wood – but both our desire to explore new

5 John Unrau, *Looking at Architecture with Ruskin*, Toronto, 1978, p. 138

possibilities, and even more, cost, must lead us to the use of new materials. But it certainly makes the life of the architect harder.

The most striking difference between the earlier buildings I have shown and the newer ones is of course the absence of decorative detail. Whatever ornament and decoration might do for our large buildings in new materials, the fact is our architects can no longer accept the legitimacy of ornamenting a building. "Ornament", John Ruskin insisted, was the essence of architecture. He was disputed on this by architects even in the mid nineteenth century: no, the essence was (as it was called then) "proportion" - namely, arrangement of space. I think we would agree that Ruskin had a rather eccentric view of the relationship between architecture and ornament. But our contemporary view is at the opposite extreme. "Ornament is crime" or "less is more" are the guiding principles of modernist architecture, of the International style, and despite a few weak efforts to modify them, they are still the prevailing practice. We may add a pyramid or dome or some other vaguely familiar form to the top of an office building, and justify it because it houses the air-conditioning or the huge blocks that limit its swaying in the wind. We will commission a sculptor to put an appropriately huge piece in the courtyard or lobby, or a weaver or ceramicist to make an enormous piece to cover the vast expanse of an office building or hotel lobby wall. But the works of art will sit there, in the lobby or on the wall, like irrelevant intrusions, linked to the building only by the simultaneity of their creation, but by nothing that organically, structurally, or aesthetically connects one with the other.

Ornament, decoration, whether the modest arrangements around doors in Georgian style that Ruskin execrated, or the elaborate structural carving that he insisted was an essential feature of building, is simply out. We might have a modest arrangement of lines in the cast concrete or cut and polished stone that make up the curtain walls of our buildings, as in William James Hall, but they will generally look silly. If we cannot get sensual satisfaction from the materials themselves – perhaps the thin slabs of stone or marble so commonly used to cover large buildings today, or the shiny metal – nothing else will be provided. Not only would it embarrass architects to design decorative detail or call for it: they wouldn't know how to do it, and there would be no craftsmen to provide it. The workmen who once carved and sculpted what seem like acres of decorated surface simply don't exist. They have been replaced by a few artists or craftsmen, whose cost is such that we can use them only for that odd piece that we stick in front of or in the lobbies of our buildings to show that we still believe in art (in any case, the government may require that a certain percentage of the cost go for art), or for restoration.

We may wonder – we should wonder – why societies that were once poorer, much poorer, than our own, could erect such elaborate structures that even maintaining them is beyond our capacities. Whatever the explanation, that is the fact. The replacement costs of our past great civic monuments would truly boggle the mind. The restoration and maintenance costs already do. One reason for this peculiar development that we would not decry is that the cost of labour, of skilled labour, has gone up relative to other costs. Our modern, democratic, industralized societies no longer reduce workmen to subsistence, as the economic theorists of the Victorian age asserted was inevitable under the pressure of economic forces. Perhaps this is the final nail in the coffin of great architecture.

So much of all this is beyond the architect's control. He is not responsible for the greater scale at which buildings must be built. He is not responsible for the flow of new materials with which he must contend. He is not responsible for the decline or disappearance of craftsmen, or for their achieving a level of income which makes their use too costly. And there is much else I have not discussed. He is not responsible for the automobile, which means that many of our great public facilities must be located within acres of parking, so that the tight weave of older cities is torn up and cannot be replaced, and which turns the entries of some of our major public complexes into holes for automobile entry rather than portals for people. He is not responsible for what seems to be a social decision simply to spend comparatively less on building. I have commented on the fact that the replacement cost of great nineteenth and early twentieth century buildings would boggle the mind. The restoration of the Statue of Liberty cost $80 million – and recall we had available for sprucing up this great monument modern inventions, such as cranes and power tools and helicopters, which the original builders did not. The restoration of the entry building at Ellis Island – built by government for utilitarian purposes – cost $140 million. What would its original cost in contemporary dollars have been? The restoration of Grand Central Station in New York City will cost $400 million. What would it cost to build anew?

Dictators can decree enormous and costly structures: democratic leaders cannot, and responsible business leaders today, dependent on shareholders and banks, and threatened by takeover artists, cannot either. Whether it was that earlier stages of our society valued certain things, like religious and public buildings, more highly; or were so arranged politically and socially that élite leaders could impose these enormous costs without restraints; or whether it was that the cost–benefit calculus which we use today for everything – the size of our defence establishment, or the relative benefit of roads and public transit, or jails and rehabilitation – simply wasn't available or wasn't considered suitable: for whatever reason, our attitudes to costs are different. When the Bishop of New York wanted to complete the Cathedral of St. John the Divine, built on traditional principles and designed to be the largest Gothic Cathedral in the world, he was much attacked: why not spend the money on the poor and homeless? He found an ingenious response: he would take unemployed poor and minority youngsters from the neighbourhood and train them to be stonecutters! (He had to import master stonecutters from England to start the process). It was still considered an eccentric decision.

Because he cannot control so many features which determine our building today, the architect or architectural critic is very often tempted to become a social reformer – as Ruskin did, or as Lewis Mumford did. Since it is society that decrees large scale, new materials, the decay of craftsmanship, modest costs for public uses, let us rebuild society. A great temptation: but in a democratic society the architect, even if he conceives himself as a prince, has no greater right or power to reform society than anyone else, and less mandate than our political leaders.

But the architect does not get off the hook that easily if we try to understand contemporary failures in public building. The architect today, in addition to his responsibility for the functional aspect of building, aims at seeing himself as an artist, as he indeed always did. Perhaps he sees himself as an artist even more today because so much of the responsibility for construction is in the hands of other professionals. If he sees himself as an artist, he must be influenced by the contemporary understanding of what an artist is, that is, one who expresses an individual vision. This reflects what has happened to art generally. The modern sculptor or painter, even when he works with public funds on a public commission, does not want to compromise his individual vision, even if it is incomprehensible to others. If he is well enough known, he need not compromise it.

The architect as artist worked well enough when architects worked within traditions that limited and guided them. These traditions were expressed in the dominant style of the time. They imposed restraint; but they guaranteed that whatever came out would achieve large acceptance, because these traditions were also familiar to the élites that made decisions, and to the people that used buildings. These traditions simply don't exist any more. For the serious architect every new major commission is a temptation to shape a new vision. He responds like the painter or sculptor, expressing himself, and is rather disdainful of those who don't understand the new vision, the new form, the new shape. And thus we have the disorder and confusion that recent work at Harvard exemplifies.

We can tolerate the varied forms of personal vision and expression of the painter or sculptor – we can look at his creations or pass them by. (Unless they obtrude upon us, whether we will or not, as in the case of some particularly objectionable contemporary public sculpture). We cannot be as indifferent to the individual vision of the architect. It may conflict with the individual vision of the architect who put up the last building – of a different material, or scale. The architect with a strong commitment to his vision for the most part simply turns his back on the fact that there are other buildings there, and this contributes to making as disorderly and disorganised a city as we have ever seen.

So much has changed: but much also remains the same, and it is this that justifies some consideration and respect for the examples of the past, when we lived in societies more ordered by restraint. In the public life, many functions are still conducted at the same scale as a hundred years ago, indeed in antiquity. The trial still involves a relatively small number of actors, and we still limit the number of observers present. The classroom and auditorium are still what they were. The deliberative assembly has not increased in size to keep up with the numbers of citizens. The same chambers that served the state a hundred years ago can serve it today. Fifty or a hundred thousand could gather in Rome for their spectacles; and the same number gather today in our cities for ours, and very much, one would think, for the same reasons. Whatever the impact of distant viewing through television, there is an excitement in the actual presence of our fellow human beings that ensures we will always have an audience for games and contests, athletic as well as political.

The main reason we gather in public spaces is for commerce – to buy, to sell, to display, to bargain, and this was true in the great cities we built in the past as it is today. This is a different use of public space from that required by the public business of the state, demanding different structures, serving different functions, but it has become the dominant form of public building today. The buildings we put up for our commercial and business functions shape the centres of our cities, whether Boston or Melbourne, and one suspects that business and commerce, private functions, simply play a much greater role in our lives than they once did. Where churches and city halls and capitals once dominated the skylines of our cities, office buildings now do. We can only admire those earlier skylines in engravings or photographs, or in a few preserved earlier cities.

We are commercial societies and it is not surprising that we allow so much of the creation of our public space to be dominated by commercial interests. However, this need not lead to inferior public space, or space indifferent to public needs. Indeed, private interests may build more extravagantly than the public builds for itself. The extravagance can be justified by the argument that it attracts more customers or clients or tenants. Further, the public, through the increasingly complex system of public controls, through the numerous powers public authorities have to safeguard the environment, in effect plays a role in determining design. The public can bargain with the private interests to get the space that it seems unwilling to provide for itself by direct taxation. It can trade off permission to build higher for public arcades or theatres, as is done in New York City and elsewhere, and there is no evidence that these means of getting public space lead to more poorly designed or less useful public space than direct public measures. (They may contribute to a crowding and overbuilding that is detrimental, but the public has power to remedy this, too, for it is public zoning allowances that set the floor on the basis of which the private builder bargains with the public authorities for the right to build more).

If we are unhappy with our public space, its quantity and its quality, we must look into ourselves for the remedy. The private builder builds with our permission. It is our own representatives who determine what facilities to provide for themselves and for us. However one struggles with the problem of public architecture, it is hard to escape from the conclusion that the answer to improving it is in the raising of public taste. However well kings or despots or robber barons or civic aristocracies may have done in the past, we don't have them any more in our Western democratic societies. (And where they still exist, they in no way create marvels of public architecture). Taste is the final arbiter – and it is the taste not only of architects and their direct clients, of elected leaders, appointed officials, private corporations, but of the public in general, which can intervene today so easily at so many places in the process of planning and design.

The education and raising of taste seems like an unimaginably difficult task – and yet it has happened. One of the ways in which we can demonstrate that it can happen is that it has, as in the example of the preservation movement. Would it be possible to tear down Pennsylvania Station in New York today? Hardly. We have financial benefits for remodelling historic landmarks we did not have in 1963, which has permitted the restoration and re-use of huge nineteenth century and early twentieth century railroad stations; we have new means of legal intervention, as was demonstrated in the successful suit to prevent a tower from being placed on top of Grand Central Station; and supporting both we have a public that appreciates architecture more, even if it can be bamboozled and confused by publicity and false authority. We have, as another example of the raising of taste, well-written architectural guides to almost every major city in the United States. Hard as it may be to believe, there were no such guidebooks to American cities thirty years ago. It was as if only Europe had architecture, and we had only structures for temporary use that it was not worth recording and appreciating. Indeed, this aspect of the education of taste has worked so well that it is now a toss-up whether we do not appreciate the buildings of the past too much, making it difficult to adapt our cities to the present.

Admittedly it is easier to educate public taste to the virtues of the past – the buildings after all are already there, and the appreciations have already been written –than to educate it to make decisions for the future.

We are left with our greatest difficulty in public building. We can appreciate and preserve the buildings of the past. But how do we build for our public functions today? We have abandoned the language of classical architecture, of pediments and columns, which served to indicate great public functions in Western architecture for 2,500 years. Occasionally forgotten or decried, this architectural language returned again and again, to serve as the symbol of our greatest aspirations in public life. We seem to have no replacement. The faint-hearted and briefly lived effort to remind us of those classical elements in "post-modernist" architecture was entirely unsatisfying, though it was sometimes entertaining. It built stage sets, which looked as if they would have no longer life than stage-sets.

We can preserve the buildings of the past. We can't build them again. The language of the past can be admired and studied, its loss can be, and is regretted, but too much has changed for it to serve us today. We are suspended between a language that cannot be used, and a language – the language of modernism – that is unsatisfying for major public purposes, but for which we have no replacement.

I think the first steps towards a more satisfactory language have been taken. We have developed a proper respect for the achievements in public building of the past. We have become emboldened in criticising the failures in public building of Modernism. But whether contemporary architects can move toward and develop a more satisfactory language for public architecture is the great question.

We can find the words to describe the building we want. In one formulation – that of Daniel P. Moynihan, writing for a committee dealing with the mundane problem of providing Federal office space thirty years ago: "the policy shall be to provide... facilities in an architectural style and form that will reflect the dignity, enterprise, vigour, and stability of the American national government". Grand words. They would serve of course also for Australia. But can we find the physical form that embodies them?

THE PUBLIC ARCHITECTURE OF AN AUSTRALIAN CITY: THE MAYOR'S CONTRIBUTION

Sallyanne Atkinson

I was going to start my presentation with the same attitude of humility that Nathan Glazer had, and say how overwhelmed I was to be here in such great company; but after Claudio Véliz's introduction, perhaps I should retract the humility. However, I do feel somewhat humble to be in the presence of so much intellect and knowledge of architecture in all its forms.

I would particularly like to be able to meet Kevin White, who is a former Mayor of Boston and a person whom I have been quoting for many years. I once read a wonderful story about him that may or may not be true, and he is going to tell me, I hope, after this. He was reported as saying that there are only two things you need to say to win votes in Boston. The first is that all Ireland must be free and the second that Trieste belongs to Italy. If nothing else, this *Conversazione* has enabled me to be here and find out if I have been misquoting him all these years.

Actually, after today, I am going to be quoting you, Nathan, because you did say some wonderful things in your presentation this morning, and like all good politicians I am ready to soak up and spread some of your ideas.

I think this is very much what a *Conversazione* is all about and I should like to congratulate you, Claudio, because I think it is very much your brain-child – something you have been hosting in Melbourne for some time, which has now gone international. Those of you who come from places outside Australia may not know that conversation as one of the great art forms is not really held in very high regard in this country. It has been something of a sadness to me in my political career that politicians who feel they ought to contribute to the great debate on the issues of our time tend to find those contributions instantly dismissed as political point-scoring, and so they withdraw to a safe position. So conversation is not considered as one of the pre-requisites of public life, and perhaps it ought to be. After all, you have gathered us here to talk, to discuss and to address ourselves to one of the very great issues of our day.

In fact I was thinking along those lines last week when I was dreaming peace-fully in one of the great cathedrals in Brisbane, St Stephen's, at a service to mark the opening of the Law Year. I was not actually away in another world, but certainly had only one ear to the sermon when I heard the Archbishop of Brisbane, Archbishop Rush, mention the word conversation, so I came back down to earth. Because I think it is important to our discussions, I might read you some extracts from what he said. He said:

> ... for Australia to be united and civilised it must share a common will to justice and equity. I believe also that it must be capable of conversation. The need for such conversation is more imperative the more complex Australian society becomes.

> On the occasion of some social turmoil thirteen years ago, with the leaders of three other churches, I made a public statement that debate marred by intemperate language contributes nothing to the meeting of minds. It only increases division. We went on to say that it is our hope that public debate be conducted with the sobriety and maturity that befits citizens of a freedom-loving democracy. I was surprised at the time and it still astonishes me, that there seemed such little public support for such a proposition.

> Someone has defined barbarism as the lack of reasonable conversation according to reasonable laws. When people cease to talk together in a reasonable fashion, one fears for civilisation. Discussion becomes uncivilised when reason is subdued by passion, when judgement is replaced by prejudice and when dialogue gives way to diatribe.

Those are the words of the Roman Catholic Archbishop of the City of Brisbane and I think it is tremendous to have approval from the Church for what you are trying to do, and more power to your elbow as you continue to do it.

We are here to address an important topic, The Public Face of Architecture. I am very aware of my technical limitations in this field. The Brisbane City Council, as some of you will of course know, is the largest local authority in this country and it does have full, and I believe proper, planning powers for the City of Brisbane. For the last five years I have chaired both the Planning Policy Committee and the Civic Cabinet, the City's decision-making committee. So I guess I do have some technical expertise or perhaps non-technical expertise.

I happen to be the mother of an architecture student and I have had many deep and meaningful discussions along the lines of, "what is architecture?" I also contributed not a little to the debate among the students of our city about whether or not architecture is art. I said I don't believe architecture is an art form. You can imagine how that went down! I also said that I don't believe architecture is an academic exercise, that it is more than designing individual buildings on drawing boards in studies and offices. I believe that architecture is very much something that affects people's lives and how they live and indeed the future of society. I believe in that connection, and so I am very much in tune with what Ruskin had to say in that regard. I think that perhaps my qualifications as an arts graduate with majors in history and political science may have qualified me to have read Ruskin's text, but I'm not quite sure whether they qualify me to actually make observations on it. But I should say, quite unashamedly, that I see my role today as making a contribution as someone who is actively involved in the effects of architecture as well as the implementation of the architectural profession.

I see my role as Lord Mayor as that of somebody nurturing and guiding our city, ensuring the health, wealth, the well-being and the moral temperature if you like, of society and the people who live in the City of Brisbane. I make my contribution, I believe, as somebody who has been in the business of cities, the places where most Australians live. About 85% of the people of this nation live in urban communities and about 63% of those live in our capital cities. I make this contribution specifically as the Lord Mayor of Brisbane, where almost one million Queenslanders have their hopes and aspirations, their disappointments and despair, where they are born, raise their family, carry out their life's work and eventually die.

A city like ours, like any other, is a combination of hills and rivers and streets and trees, and in Brisbane's case, it is made special by the way our river winds its way through our hills and trees that flower and are bright with colour all through the year. The fact is, we have a climate that allows people to live their lives outdoors. That is what gives Brisbane a special atmosphere, a special personality, a special character and therefore affects the lives of the people who live in it and the shape of its buildings.

The city is a total of its buildings and its buildings are the landmarks that give it identity. If we think of Paris, we think of boulevards and buildings and the Eiffel Tower, and if we think of London we think of St Paul's. If we think of Rome, we think of its great churches, and when I think of Brisbane I think of old Queensland houses and the large buildings like the Treasury Building. Buildings are what give people pride in their city and when people are proud of their city, they work harder, they have a greater commitment to making the city a good place to be. All the other things, the things that we do, such as building roads, parks, gardens, libraries, all those very important aspects of local government, are very much dependent on the commitment and enthusiasm of the people.

I'm going to address today four points that I think need to be discussed in our consideration of the Public Face of Architecture. The first is the quality of the buildings themselves. This is of course something that is highly subjective and something architects tend to talk a lot about. It is something that is very much dependent on public taste, but it is very much in the hands of the architects, and one thing I say to groups of architects who I am frequently called upon to address is that they do have a responsibility to go out and do well and to influence public taste. Architects, particularly those in private practice, will say to you and me that, "Well of course, you know, it's what the client wants". When I say to them "Why the hell did you do it. It's so awful". They say, "That's what the client wants, we're really in the hands of the marketplace". I do think the architectural profession has a responsibility to set the agenda, to create an atmosphere of well being. I don't think people really want to make a choice, they want to be told what is good.

Of course in Brisbane, and I'm sure here and even in Boston, we have all kinds of fashions. In architecture we have gone through that fad where we had little blue triangles and circles on the tops of buildings, or the one where all buildings had to be pink or blue or apricot. What happens is that someone puts up a building and everybody says, "Well, I'll have another one like that". There is a marked lack of imagination, a lack of courage if architects allow this to happen.

The next point I would like to make is the importance of how buildings relate to each other. Of course I am talking from the point of view of somebody who is responsible for a whole city, and with the knowledge that to those within the city, how buildings relate to each other is very important. A few years ago Brisbane went through a massive public debate about tall buildings and at about this time I visited Houston, Texas and saw some wonderful tall buildings. They were wonderful, of course, in the way they related to each other. When you stood back from the skyline it looked like a sculpture. These buildings, like the Johnson building for example, were not only of great merit individually, but the way in which they were connected was very important.

A couple of months ago I was in Jerusalem at a conference of Mayors there. The thing that struck me was how all the buildings in Jerusalem are all built of one fabric, Jerusalem stone. I must say the first day I was there, I thought, "Oh, everything here is olive green and sand and there is very little colour". But in fact once you get used to it it's not so bad and the people of Jerusalem think it's wonderful, and pointed out with great pride the fact that all their buildings are built with the same thing.

I think how buildings contribute to a city as a whole is very important. Buildings, public buildings particularly, need to make some kind of statement about the city and in fact about the time in which they were built. The nicest tall building we have in the City of Brisbane at the moment is the Central Plaza Building, which just happens to have been built by a Japanese architect. I'm not quite sure if that is going to make some statement in years to come about the Japanese involvement in Brisbane, Queensland, Australia at that time. That is really incidental to the fact that I think the building contributes very well to the city skyline.

As I mentioned earlier, a couple of years ago we did have a great and fiery public debate, when a developer, (who happens to come from Melbourne), wanted to build in our city the world's tallest building of 107 storeys. The public said "Hey, hey, hey, we don't like it". A lot of other people, mainly engineers and architects, I must say, said, "You have to have progress, you have to move forward, it's going to be a wonderful building". Engineers told me it was going to introduce the latest of technology inside – wonderful lifts and innovative ways of putting down foundations. Apart from anything else, it was just totally out of scale, as you can imagine, in a city of our size with the buildings we have. Our tallest building is 48 storeys and this building would have been 107 storeys. It would have thrown the whole symmetry of the city out of kilter. The Council was taken to court for refusing the application and I found myself having a very interesting time in front of a judge. The prosecution case was based on the fact that I made public statements saying I didn't like the building before it had gone through proper Council process. I said to the Judge that I thought my role as the elected Mayor of the city was, in fact, to make statements and make judgements. The judge apparently agreed with me because we actually won the case.

My favourite public building is the Queensland Treasury Building. It is a very large stone building in the heart of the city which is often described as the finest example of Italian Renaissance architecture in the Southern Hemisphere. I'm not quite sure where the others are. It was built in 1885 at a time when Brisbane and Queensland were very, very small indeed. In fact, when Queensland became a State about 25 years before, there was only seven and a half pence in the State Treasury and that was stolen three days later. But the people of that time had confidence in their city and enough pride to build a building of this kind and to do it very well. It's a beautiful building, not only because it is nicely in proportion, but it also makes use of architectural features that are important to us, like big windows, arches and balconies suited to the Queensland climate.

I think that buildings contributing to the city as a whole should have something of the special character of that city. I think it's rather alarming when we see buildings all over the world looking the same. I think we are now seeing acceptance that individualism by identity is very important and I certainly believe that the buildings that we want to see in our city should have a special Queensland, Brisbane flavour. You should be able to say about Brisbane, as you can about Boston, for example, that these are buildings that are right for their own sake and indeed right for their time.

Another aspect that is very important, and I think Ruskin touched on that in the moral connection, is how buildings make people feel. How the buildings affect the lives of the people who live there and how they affect the people who walk around those cities. The human face of architecture if you like.

It has always surprised me that more attention is not paid to the architecture of school buildings. Children spend a large percentage of their lives in those buildings, which are generally large, chunky, institutional collections of brick, concrete and stone. I believe that far too little attention is paid to the fact that buildings in which a young person is going to spend his or her formative years are going to make a great deal of difference to those children.

We are seeing a whole new dimension to this debate on architecture. It is great that people like Prince Charles are buying into it, because he was able to get out and say things that the politicians wouldn't dare say. He was able to say things that ordinary individuals wouldn't have had the confidence to say. He could say them and know that attention was going to be paid to him because he is the Prince of Wales. It shows me, at least, that the British have a royalty prepared to think, and I believe that it's very important indeed to have the courage of conviction. I don't think it much matters whether he is right or wrong and I viewed with some interest the coverage of the debate that followed. Architects, taking themselves very seriously indeed, asked how he could say these things. I don't think it matters a damn what he said. To me, the important thing is that he's actually saying it and that people are thinking about it and replying.

We have reached a stage where people are much more aware of their own quality of life and much more prepared to get up and say what they think. Perhaps it's that people are much better educated; and they certainly are better educated on a broader spectrum of things. On the other hand, we now have a situation where everyone thinks they are an expert. They think that because they watch a lot of television, and they read the newspapers, that they know a lot about a lot, and I think that's a fairly dangerous trend in a sense. There is a great danger in allowing the public voice to be heard too much, because we all know, that the voice that gets heard the loudest is not necessarily the best voice. Now, in fact, to be labelled as a proper expert on something is almost to be accused of being in an ivory tower. So I think it's very important that people such as yourselves, people who do have knowledge and expertise have the courage and confidence to back up that expertise and indeed, to stand by it.

I thought I might just talk a little about changing trends in architecture and changing public attitudes to it. I remember when I was growing up, Robin Boyd was a great authority on everything architectural. I read once that he described domestic architecture in Australia as the "Story of material triumph and aesthetic calamity". He was talking mainly about houses, and many of the characteristics he most disdained are now found in Queensland houses. These same houses are now greatly prized by the people who live in our city and those that visit, and I rather like this excerpt from Boyd's book, *Australia's Home*.

> The galvanised iron roofs on their front verandas dipped in a sudden curve like the brim of a sundowner's hat and were draped at the edge with cast iron, like corks on a brim to frighten away the flies.

I don't think he was being complimentary. He, of course, lived between the 1920s and 70s and his views were the views of many people during that period when Australia was suffering from a cultural cringe, and a belief that Australia could not be Australian and be good. We went through a time when many old and historically significant buildings were demolished to make way for the glass and concrete monoliths that back then spoke of progress and worldliness.

I remember in fact, when I was newly elected to Council 12 years ago, I was amazed that nobody was doing anything about preserving these old suburban houses. I went to see the Lord Mayor of the day, who was an older man, not of my party and talked to him about it. He said "What would you want to save those horrible little wooden houses for? Everyone wants to live in brick houses now". He came to me about two years later and said, "I think you may be right". He said his son had just come up from Sydney and wanted to be taken to the house in which his dad was born. A terrible old house the Mayor said it was. A terrible old wooden house with a corrugated iron roof. His son from Sydney thought this was wonderful, and of course we are seeing this all the time now, and these houses are preserved and loved.

Most of these buildings, which are not old at all really by European or even American standards, are valuable, not just for their age, but for the fact that they do tell us something about Australia's history, about our heritage and about the ingenuity of the people who settled in this country. It is good for our children to be able to go to some of these old homes that are now museums, where they can actually walk in and have a look at the household equipment that the early women used. The children are overwhelmed by what people had to put up with in those days. No television and no washing machine. I think that's very important because it does give us a sense of pride in our past, and from that pride in our past comes the confidence of the future. It was Walter Burley Griffin who said that:

> Buildings are the most subtle, accurate and enduring records of life. Hence, their problems are the problems of life and not problems of form. But through the form and material of buildings we can gain an insight into the life of the past.

Brisbane in one sense has been very fortunate, because for a very long time we were looked on as the country-cousin of everything that happened in the rest of Australia. Brisbane was seen as a large country town, kind of quaint, but nothing to write home about. We benefited, in fact, from being kept in a state of suspended animation for many years, because by the time we were ready to take off and to develop and grow, other places had made mistakes from which we were able to learn. We were also able to pick up, copy and learn from the best of what other places had done. So while we have had our share of those bland, boring and ugly buildings that we have talked about, we have not been left with as many as some. At least when Brisbane's building boom began, people were certainly aware of the importance of a building relating to its surroundings and of other things like the importance of greenery and trees.

We are now incorporating in our city's buildings those common sense features, like shaded walkways to block out the summer sun. We are using more verandas and trees in our dwellings and public buildings. We are seeing the sorts of things that went missing for quite some time.

In fact, I found the other day a fairly telling item in a Brisbane City Council publication of 1974 which showed a picture of some old houses in the City, overshadowed by an enormous concrete monstrosity. It was with pride the Council reported that:

> ...these old homes, many of them built in the latter part of the nineteenth century, are gradually disappearing from the Brisbane scene. Their place is being taken by modern high-rise office blocks such as the Main Roads Commission Building in the background.

Any of you who have seen the Main Roads Commission Building in Brisbane would know that it's not something of which to be particularly proud.

By some miracle, as though the alarm had been perfectly timed, Brisbane awoke with many of her original features intact, many of her public buildings in place, and to find that people now have become very interested in the architecture of our ancestors and in architecture generally. Once upon a time, people were embarrassed by the funny little houses on stilts that Robin Boyd described in such a derogatory way. Now they are considered very much a part of Brisbane's character and very much a part of what we want to preserve and indeed emulate.

In fact, as part of the public participation process, we in the Council have recently put out some design guidelines which were intended for developers and architects. They have in fact, been taken up and asked for by individual members of the community who are writing back to us with their comments about what we are suggesting. We are careful, of course, not to introduce too many regulations for architects and developers. I don't want to cramp imagination in any sense at all. It is also very important that we don't automatically adopt these ideas exactly as they were then, because they were ideas that were right for their own time. People were building verandas because it made a lot of sense, but they were also using materials because they were all they had available. I must say that just because all old houses in Brisbane were painted a nasty yellow ochre colour, it doesn't mean that if you're restoring those houses you have to paint them a nasty yellow ochre colour.

A few years ago, I got into some mild trouble with the National Trust, of which I was Vice President at the time and am now Patron and Life Member. In Brisbane we have the only City Hall in Australia. All the other capital cities have town halls because ours was built in 1930, long after the other ones, when Brisbane had already become a city. When we restored the interior of City Hall, they wanted me to do paint-scraping and go back to the original colours. Now City Hall was built at the beginning of the depression. They couldn't afford to do anything and it was quite horrendous, dingy and depressing. I have restored it in the way they would have liked to have done it if they could.

Another building of which I'm fond, which isn't really a building at all but a structure, is the Storey Bridge. We recently celebrated the 50th anniversary of the Bridge, which was a wonderful celebration. The Storey Bridge was begun in 1935 at the height of the depression. It is the second largest bridge in Australia and the largest engineering structure of its time in the world, which again shows the kind of confidence and courage there was at the time. It is also a shape that is familiar to people and symbolic of Brisbane - a structure that has contributed to the life of the city.

I would like to sum up by saying that I speak here today, not as an expert in architecture. I think it is very important that I say to all of you professionals from all of your different spheres, "Don't be too academic". When you are thinking about what is the right thing to do, remember that it's the people out there who will use those buildings, who will look at those buildings, whose feelings about their cities and communities, about what they believe they themselves can do, will be very much affected by those buildings and their contribution to the city.

Can I also say to you that I think we have a heavy responsibility to stand up and say what we think about design, and what is good design and good architecture. We have to go out and market those ideas in the community so that people know and understand. I believe there is a great yearning out there for quality, understanding and knowledge. People basically want to do the right thing and they're just not too sure what the right thing is. I think that those of us in political life have a great responsibility to keep talking to you, and to keep having conversations of this sort. I'm delighted to have been part of this one.

SOME PRINCIPLES OF VERNACULAR ARCHITECTURE

Roger Scruton

My subject belongs to the criticism, rather than the philosophy, of architecture. However, many of the errors in architectural practice have philosophical roots, and naïve and undiscerning philosophies of man have been impatiently transcribed into the critical language and practical maxims of modern building. From time to time, therefore, I shall cast an eye into the philosophical depths beneath the questions that concern me.

There is a special need in architecture for publicly accepted canons of taste. Buildings may be commissioned by individual clients, but they are encountered by the entire public, and all of us have an interest in their appearance. To build is to impose yourself on others, and therefore to awaken their appraisal: criticism is as appropriate a response to building, therefore, as it is to the morality or manners by which others live. It is not enough for an architect to say "I like it"; or even "I and my educated colleagues like it". He has to *justify its existence*, and the question is whether he and his colleagues are right.

In the public and decorative arts, the search for some kind of co-ordination of tastes is therefore forced on us by our nature as social beings. This search may not lead to a single set of principles; nevertheless it involves a common pursuit of an acceptable solution. Aesthetic values in architecture must form part of a solution to a "co-ordination problem", and cannot be construed in the purely individualistic and expressionist manner that is familiar to us from discussions of modern painting and music. We must fit our house to our neighbour's house if we are to live together peacefully – even if we also live, as John Rawls puts it, in a state of "mutual unconcern".

Perhaps one of the most instructive instances of what I mean is provided by the Georgian terrace. Here a common style and a yielding civility of manner offer a rational solution to the problem of co-existence. The solution emerges, we might add, by an "invisible hand", from the work of many different builders and in response to the demands of many different clients. (Figure 1 shows Kennington Park Road, whose undistinguished character is precisely what endears us to it.) Such an aesthetic solution also provided the glory of the Victorian slums, which the modern obsession with hygiene and eugenics caused us so thoughtlessly to destroy.

Fig.1 Terrace houses, Kennington Park Road, London

Georgian terraces and Victorian slums bring me to my theme, which is vernacular architecture: the architecture of the ordinary builder, the man with neither pretension nor claim to genius, who has nevertheless availed himself of patterns and principles through which to exercise his taste, to please his clients, and to make lasting decisions as to what is right and wrong. It is my view that we should pay far more attention to the vernacular in architecture than to the masterpieces of the art; for it is through this everyday practice that the most important aesthetic problems are solved, that architecture acquires its meaning for us, and that our real values find expression.

Through aesthetic reflection we endeavour to create a world in which we are at home with others and with ourselves: and home is not home without the implication of community. If there is a single philosophical idea that underpins the practice of the vernacular architect, it lies here – in the idea of home. Man's "estrangement" in the modern city is due to many causes besides modern ways of building. But who can deny that these modern ways have played their own special part in producing it, by adopting forms, masses, materials and proportions which bear no relation to our aesthetic expectations, and which arrogantly defy the wisdom and achievement of the past? Home is not occupied only by us: it is inhabited by the ghosts of our ancestors, and by the premonition of children who are yet to be. Its essence is continuity, and it provides the archetype of every experience of peace.

The failings of Modernism are to be witnessed less in its grandiose projects and striking novelties than in its patterns: the architectural elements which get into the hands of the talentless and uninstructed, and which, repeated *ad nauseam* in every modern city, ensure that we find no resting place, but are everywhere homeless and insecure. The typical vernacular construction in the modern style is composed at the drawing board. It consists in an accumulation of horizontal slabs, without vertical movement, with no mouldings, details or expression, with no concluding pinnacle or battlement, slapped like a fist into the city sky. It is not that such a building is ill-proportioned and on the wrong scale: the same could be said of many an ordinary Georgian house. It is that its language is uncouth, unredeemed by life or detail, utterly indifferent to its surroundings, or to the person who is obliged to pass by the building.

What was wrong with Modernism was not its rigidity, its moralising, its puritanical zeal – although these were repulsive enough. Modernism's respect for discipline was its sole redeeming feature; but it was a discipline about the *wrong things*. It told us to be true to function, to social utility, to materials, to political principles. It told us to be "of our time", while enlisting architecture in those insolent experiments for the re-fashioning of man which have threatened our civilisation with such disaster. At the same time Modernism threw away, as a worthless by-product of the past and a symbol of its oppressive rituals, the *aesthetic* discipline embodied in the Gothic and classical traditions. It had no use for *that* kind of discipline, and no patience towards the few brave critics who defended it, as the only discipline that counts.

Modernism should be compared, I believe, to bolshevism – with which it was, for a while, associated, both in the work of the Russian constructivists, and in the Bauhaus under the leadership of Hannes Meyer. Modernism, like bolshevism, was a bid for liberation, beginning in bold experiment, but exacting an enormous regimentation, the final legacy of which was a complete loss of the freedom that was coveted, and of the discipline without which freedom has no sense. The true legacy of Modernism does not lie in those eccentric lumps of concrete which are scattered around the countryside of Europe, and which receive such reverential commentary in textbook after textbook. It lies in the building types which compose what I call the "horizontal style" – the style which derives directly from the drawing board, and which is based on no discipline of the mind, the soul or the eye. This is the vernacular of Modernism, and it provides a very good illustration of my theme. For it shows why the vernacular in architecture is so much more important than the models from which it derives.

The builders of Georgian London were, for the most part, simple people who designed from pattern books. These books derived ultimately from the great Renaissance and post-Renaissance treatises, such as those of Alberti, Serlio and Palladio, and enshrined what might reasonably be called a tradition of practical thinking. The forms had shown their adaptability, and their ability to answer to the recurrent problems of the builder – not the narrowly utilitarian problems only, but those aesthetic problems in which the humanity of a building is put to the test. One such problem is that posed by the door of a house. The door is the point of transition between inner and outer, private and public. It should be polite, dignified, like any outward manifestation of the inner life; it should also be prominent and welcoming. And it should be interesting without being eccentric, embellishing the street but on no account disrupting it with vulgar self-display. The classical pattern books offered the builder a variety of solutions to this problem, all of them tried and accepted; each of them was easy to reproduce, and required neither talent nor skill beyond what could be expected of the ordinary builder.

Fig. 2 Neoclassical doorway designs

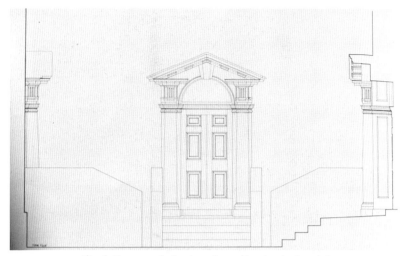

Fig. 3 Doorway design based on a Neoclassical model

(Figures 2 and 3 give two archetypes, the first noble and close to the Renaissance originals, the second worn away, rounded and adapted by a century or more of agreeable pretence.)

It is, I am sure, hardly necessary to remind you of the disaster of the door in the modernist building types. The horizontal style in fact makes no place for doors, so that the juncture between inner and outer remains always vaguely defined – sometimes an invisible slit in a screen of glass, sometimes squeezed helplessly into corners, opening onto some arbitrarily defined space, presenting neither an invitation to enter nor a promise of security. Worse still is the habit of concealing the door altogether, so that each house, even when joined in a terrace, turns its back completely on its neighbour.

If I were to express in a word what it is that so many modern buildings lack, the word I should choose is "civility". This lack of civility is not a superficial thing; on the contrary, it goes to the heart of life in the modern world. Civility is the virtue that fits man for society: it consists in the ability to adjust to one's neighbour, to meet him on terms, even when the terms are unequal, and to strive gently but firmly for peaceful dealings in the midst of contest and conceit. It is a necessary virtue, for the reason that we are social beings, who become what we truly are only in the condition of society. Without the virtue of civility we acquire neither the public existence which defines our field of action, nor the private life in which we are consoled.

Fig. 4 Sir Denys Lasdun, Institute of Education, University of London.

Fig. 5 View of Tavistock Square, towards Lasdun's Institute of Education

Buildings are like people in this and also in many another respect. They too acquire their nature from their participation in, and collective creation of, a public realm, against which their private spaces are defined, and into which their varied life is poured. Civility in architecture, as in all human life, is the art of the boundary: the art of defining the place where public and private meet, and of ensuring that the line remains permeable to the commerce between them. As with human morality, this virtue arises in architecture from the corporate attempt to live by agreement. The uncivil building offers no clear boundary between inner and outer; it turns its back on the world, and is conceived in terms of one horizontal gesture which sweeps away the negotiated verticals that are the hallmark of the classical orders, and of the vernacular tradition that derived from them. An appropriate illustration is Figure 4, showing Sir Denys Lasdun's Institute of Education in the University of London, a building as repulsive as the activities that are contained in it. This building is usefully compared with the Georgian Order that stands next to it: Tavistock Square (Fig. 5), which gives a clear indication not only of the elements of civility, but also of the ability of the Georgian builder to provide them. It is important to notice that the Order of this terrace is primarily vertical. Although the horizontal movement is marked and emphatic, it arises by repetition, and is derived from vertical columns and pilasters linked in a chain. However long this chain, the building seems always to stand and face the passer-by, providing a discreet civil background to his movement, just as people do.

The Classical Order, from which the Georgian vernacular stems, was conceived as a single vertical section: base, column and architrave, the parts, details and proportions of which could be explained completely without reference to the whole composition, much as one explains a harmony in music. The Order was the primary unit of design, a complete vertical element, all the details of which were visually comprehended within the upward movement. Plinth, cornice, entablature, column, capital and mouldings serve not merely to mark out the proportions of the walls and to bear the structure of the roof: they also divide the unit into intelligible sections, investing it with light, shade and contrast, so that the proportions become visible, and the relations defined. The art of building can be taught through the study of such vertical elements, but never through the study of horizontal sections or ground plans. The Order defines and explores a posture, imitating the human frame and answering to our ways of seeing it. The discipline contained in an Order brings an immense gift of freedom: the Order can be extended sideways into colonnades, courtyards and facades; along straight lines or curves; through squares, streets or crescents. In each new arrangement its orderliness and posture are preserved. This flexibility is common to all the styles that share the vertical emphasis: the Gothic, the

Romanesque, and all other variants of the classical discipline which comes to us from Greece and Rome. By contrast, the horizontal style never acquires a posture, in whatever way it is extended: whether square or round, straight or curved, high or low, the horizontally-composed building looks characterless. The seeming freedom which the architect enjoys at the drawing board is in fact a kind of arbitrariness: not liberty but licence, not freedom but randomness and irresponsibility.

The Orders were originally associated with complex systems of measurement, and a meticulous attention to proportion. Even when questions of geometry are downgraded or ignored, however, the details of the Orders may still be used to impose vertical posture. Indeed, it is by virtue of the mouldings, string-courses and cornices derived from the old pattern books, that the disproportionate buildings of the early twentieth century were able to stand side by side so agreeably: as we can easily witness in Lower Manhattan. And one of the most remarkable effects of the classical details lies in their ability to join a building – whatever its height and grandeur – to the street from which it rises, creating a place of dialogue on the pavement.

Reflecting on the Orders, and the tradition that contains them, we can arm ourselves against one of the most disastrous of the fallacies of modernism: the geometrical theory of proportion. This theory originated in Pythagorean number symbolism, and was passed through Plato, Macrobius and Boethius to medieval aesthetics and cosmology. And the prime movers of the pattern-book tradition – Alberti, Serlio and Palladio – all paid lip-service to a view which they found already hinted at in Vitruvius, and explicitly developed in Boethius and St Augustine: the view that all harmony, acoustic or visual, can be encompassed and explained by mathematical relations. The residue of two millennia of airy speculation can be found in Le Corbusier's "modulor", in which the Greek practice of building according to repeatable measures or "modules" is given a new lease of life. If measures are arranged according to a particular mathematical pattern, Le Corbusier suggested, the overall composition will strike the eye as harmonious. Proportion resides in mathematical relations – for example, between the length and height of a wall – and can be achieved regardless of the materials, and without the details provided by the classical Orders. The Orders, too, had their geometrical discipline, the finesse of which surpasses anything envisaged by Le Corbusier. Nevertheless, their achievement does not reside in the science of measurement. On the contrary, the Orders constitute an emancipation from measurement, which is also, in a sense, an emancipation from geometry.

What I mean is this: it is fruitless for a building to be based on measurement, if the measures cannot be perceived. And they can be perceived only if a building is divided into significant parts, which can be comprehended in their isolation as well as in their unity. Harmony can be achieved only where there is also *composition*. There must be observable and significant divisions in the architectural totality – and especially vertical divisions, like those we observe (chin, shoulder, waist and ankle) in the human frame. Such divisions mark a point of transition: lines of force gather there, interact, resolve, and pass on. As a result, the divisions concentrate the life that occupies the wall-space.

The modernist style forbids mouldings, plinths, capitals and cornices: or if it allows them it is only in forms so unemphatic and shame-faced, as to make no visual impact. Instead of columns and capitals we have the unadorned pilotis – a column which comes to no conclusion, but which seems to drill invisibly through the beam it supports, passing out of sight with its tensions unconfessed and unresolved. Modernist walls are without string-courses, their windows lack proper frames, and their doorways are mere orifices. Their movement is spread sideways to infinity (cf. again Lasdun's Institute of Education), or cancelled entirely by the heaped-up layers of the horizontal style.

The Orders identify particular junctures in the wall or colonnade as points of drama and transition. Here the movement is gathered up, arrested, and then passed on with a renewed impetus. Base, capital, architrave and cornice; string-courses, plinths and attic storeys – all are picked out with shadows and given their specific character. The geometry of the building is made *perceivable*, since the lines that are related by it are endowed with a beginning, middle and end, and the whole into which they are integrated has the character of a composition, in which competing forces are resolved and harmonised.

By this very process, the need for a precise geometry is overcome. The details themselves come to acquire the marks of order, and acquire a harmonising potential that allows them to be transferred from building to building, bringing even the wildest and most erratic movement under a kind of civilised control. Once the patterns have been established, the builder has to hand a method for generating harmony *in the absence* of measure, and for perpetuating the memory of proportion in a composition by which the strict Pythagorean would probably be outraged.

Imagine a beautifully formed body – as depicted by Ingres, for example. Here we see a certain kind of perfection, in the lengths and disposition of the limbs, in the proportions of body to leg, head to neck, and so on. And imagine a purely mathematical version of this figure – the head replaced by an oval pumpkin, the legs by tubular sandbags, and what you will. The mathematical relations would remain; but the beauty would have disappeared. It would cease to be appropriate to speak of proportion. For the proportion of a figure belongs to it only as *interpreted*. It is as a *head* that the oval relates to the column upon which it rests, and as a *body* that the column relates to the head. And not just any head or body: the head and body of a young woman, in whose eye shines the light of reason, and who therefore *looks* at us out of the picture.

The mathematics of the beautifully formed body may be disturbed without doing violence to the grace and beauty, provided that the details retain their significance, and call to each other in the right tone of voice, so to speak, across the spaces that divide them. Thus, in Botticelli's *Venus* we see a most extraordinary distortion of the neck, an elongation of the arms, and a thousand departures from our common-sense anatomy. But what grace is there, nevertheless. It is just this kind of grace that may survive in the vernacular use of columns and architraves, even in the most surprising places, and detached entirely from the context that gave rise to them.

The vertical order to which I have referred is a necessary part of the construction of a public façade. One of the greatest achievements of modernism is to have destroyed the façade. Buildings like the Regent Hotel in Melbourne face in no particular direction, and offer no coherent aspect, no matching of part to part, from whatever angle they may be viewed. Modernist doors are tucked out of the way, meaninglessly and invisibly. The buildings contain no real apertures, since the distinctions between window, wallspace and door have been virtually abolished – or at any rate confused – by the use of glass screens that incorporate all of them, and elide them into a single movement. Yet, even in the absence of detailing, the classical disposition of apertures can cause a building to smile at us agreeably and to welcome our glance. And if you add to this the resources of the classical language, the varieties of expression become infinite.

Fig. 6 A modern utility corner, London

The absence of vertical order has not only destroyed the façade; it has removed from the modern building-types any ability to negotiate a street or to stand comfortably in constricted places. Modern buildings have to zig-zag around corners, in order to follow the rigid constraints of their oblong ground-plans, leaving the street to look after itself, and creating those rubbishy angles in which life expires. Figure 6 shows one such. Another instance, on a vaster scale, is provided by London's South Bank complex, from the "heroic" period of modernist architecture: a kind of wasteland of unmitigated corners.

Fig. 7 A corner at Lincoln's Inn, London

One should contrast this with the enormous resources available to the builder in the classical styles, when it comes to filling a corner, or making an interesting passage through or around it. (Figure 7 shows a cheerful little corner, not the least bit rubbishy, from Lincoln's Inn.)

Before going on to examine the classical vernacular in more detail, it is worth making a few concluding observations concerning its modernist competitor. There is perhaps no more effective way of understanding the lack of civility – the uncivilised nature – of the modernist building-types than by seeing how badly they fit to their neighbours, even when attempting to maintain a common scale. Not only do they clash with the old vernacular buildings; they also clash hideously with one another. The absence of significant detail, the cheerless mirror glass, and the regimented fenestration make it impossible for us to contemplate the juxtaposition of competing ceiling-heights without a feeling of profound revulsion. Even the scantiest use of classical mouldings – notwithstanding the fact that it may emphasise the competition of scales – serves to moderate the conflict and render it bearable. (Figure 8 shows an interesting example from Hastings.)

Fig. 8 Buildings behaving as "good neighbours", Hastings

Fig. 9 View of Leadenhall Market, London

The contrast between the old and the new vernacular is never more revealing than when they occur side by side. Figure 9 shows an undistinguished Victorian building – Leadenhall Market – behind which two modernist horrors are locked in battle, the pencil-like verticals of the one slicing through the dull horizontals of the other like dentures through a piece of discoloured angel-cake. The clash here is absolute and unmitigated. We should also contrast the phoney verticality of the modernist building on the left with the true verticality of the market, in which details accumulate one over the other, progressing harmoniously to the pinnacle that crowns their movement. It is this movement that enables the market to fit comfortably to its equally undistinguished neighbours. Here harmony and order are achieved without any special beauty, and in the absence of style.

I have attributed the vertical posture of the classical vernacular to the discipline of the Orders: the discipline involved in arranging a wall around a real or implied colonnade. As I have already argued, however, there are details derived from this discipline which have acquired the intrinsic marks of it, and which can therefore be used to give a human countenance to structures that are otherwise shapeless or ungainly. Nothing has been more important in this respect than the cornice, which causes the vertical line to break into flower at its conclusion, thereby bringing its upward movement to a fitting end. Figure 10 shows W. Curtis Green's electricity generating station at Chiswick. This building, constructed on an enormous scale, displays the fertility of the classical language. The great windows convey enormous humour, well-being, and a joyous acceptance of the surrounding world – an effect which is inseparable from the freestone voussoirs, set in brick, and the contrapuntal attic storey that emphasises their size. By such devices a plain industrial box, of great and ungainly size, has been turned into a façade of such strength and gaiety that the building has outlasted its original function, and become a constant companion to the neighbourhood. It very soon ceased to be a generating station and became a bus depot; now it is used as workshops and flats. There is a moral here for those who are tempted by utilitarian ways of thinking. It has been often said that the form of a building is, or should be, dictated by its function.

Fig. 10 W. Curtis Green, Electricity Generating Station, Chiswick

44

And of course, this is exactly what we find, in the modernist building-types. The fact is, however, that buildings last longer than their functions, which change on average every twenty years. The successful building is therefore the one which is *least* attached to its initial function, and most able to survive a change in it. And what is it that enables buildings to survive? The answer is obvious: they survive because we like the look of them. In comparison with this fact, every consideration of function dwindles into insignificance.

The cornice illustrates another principle of the classical idiom: the principle of shadow. Aesthetically speaking, buildings are not composed of brick and stone and stucco, but of light and shade. Or rather, they emerge from the interaction between the materials from which they are built, and the light in which they stand: light needs shade, as good needs evil, in order to be known. Leonardo wrote that "shadow is the display by bodies of their form; and the forms of bodies give no impression of their quality without it". The significance of a building derives, then, from the interplay of form and shadow, and the true architect must design with shadow as much as he designs with brick or stone. That is why mouldings are essential to the art of building. And it is mouldings that are the primary lesson of the pattern-books.

Figure 11 shows shadow generated within the very matter of a wall, at Lincoln's Inn, bringing the wall forward into consciousness, making it a friendly competitor for the space in which we live: a companion in commerce. From such examples you can learn much about walls: not about their structure, perhaps, but about their phenomenology. Nor is it only on sunny days that shadow outlines and articulates the details of a building. Even when light gives out entirely, mouldings may yet have a role to play, shining with rain or glimmering with a delicate coating of snow. Nor do you need to work in stone or stucco to produce these effects. The vernacular of lower Manhattan abounds in light-filled parallels, many of them achieved by the use of pressed tin. There is, of course, a real and deeply significant distinction to be made between carved and modelled forms. In the case of architecture, however, there is a far greater distinction between those who use mouldings – whether cut in stone, pressed in steel or set in plaster – and those who eschew them, under the conviction that "ornament is crime". Mouldings are the means whereby we become sculptors of shadow: and without them a building can hardly speak to us.

Fig. 11 Shadows within a wall, Lincoln's Inn, London

If you study the old pattern-books you will discover an interesting fact. In addition to showing the standard patterns and forms, they also analyse the shadows that are cast by them. Textbooks of architecture, of the kind used to train the common-or-garden builders of Melbourne or Manhattan, would contain instructions for drawing the shadows on the various parts of an Order. I doubt that you would be required either to learn or even to notice such things in a contemporary school of architecture. Indeed, if you showed too much interest in them, as did Quinlan Terry when a student at the Architectural Association, you would probably fail to qualify.

How, then, shall we define the classical vernacular? Briefly, I mean a tradition of patterns, adapted to the uses of the ordinary builder, and capable of creating accord and harmony in all the many circumstances of potential conflict. These patterns have emerged from the steady adaptation of the vertical Order –based on column, base, architrave and cornice– to the life of the modern city. The

46

ruling principle has been civility: the creation of a public world of mutual respect the boundaries of which are permeable to the private interests that are sheltered by it.

Why should we venerate this vernacular style? I shall conclude with two briefly sketched ideas in answer to that question. The first goes to the heart of architectural aesthetics. Architecture forms part of the embellishment of everyday life. Its goal is not originality or self-expression: its goal is harmony, good-will and order. Buildings ought not to be designed for the *cognoscenti*, but for the mass of mankind; and the practice of architecture does not lie in the hands of geniuses, but in those of ordinary and half-talented people, whose task is to make us feel at home. Architecture must call, therefore, upon what is widely understood, easily repeatable, and successfully combined. Its problems are far from the self-created intricacies of a Valéry or a Schoenberg; they arise naturally and inevitably just as soon as stone is laid on stone or brick on brick.

This is not to say that architectural problems are easy, or that genius is not as necessary in this art as in the concert hall and the museum. But although it requires genius to solve the problems of the builder, the solutions, once discovered, become the common property of the semi-talented. Let me give you an example. Few things are more painful to the human eye than a right-angled collision of vertical forms. The problem of the corner – and especially of the inner corner - has therefore always preoccupied serious architects, and especially those upon whom the burden of discovering a new style has fallen.

When the Renaissance architects first revived the Roman styles in order to embellish their new commercial havens and the religious sanctuaries that conjured the spirit to dwell among them, they too encountered this problem. Figure 11 gives an example from S. Marco in Rome in which the architect's beautiful idea, of crowning each arc with a little console of stone, has served only to emphasise the catastrophic collision at the corner. The two columns of the Ionic Order above are locked in mortal combat, chafing away at each other's protruding details like foolish quarrelling old men. The solution to this conflict had been already discovered 150 miles away by Brunelleschi; fifty years later it reached Rome. It was necessary to replace the full column by a buried column, graced by pilasters, so that the vertical member upon which the corner pivots ceases to be visible. The Order is now imagined by the perceiver, buried in the masonry like the sculptor's figure within his block of stone. (Figure 12 shows the effect, in another courtyard at S. Marco.) The solution shows the immense imaginative power of the Orders. They exert their influence even when they are not really there, but merely implied by the visible skin of a building.

Fig. 12 Collision in a corner, S. Marco, Rome

Such a solution requires genius for its discovery. Once discovered, however, it can be incorporated into the pattern-book, reproduced in standard parts, and indeed made on a lathe for the use of every builder, as in Georgian London. This probably is not, but nevertheless ought to be, what Kant meant when, in the *Critique of Judgment*, he wrote that "Genius is the innate mental disposition through which nature gives the rule to art". Is that not the right way to proceed? And do we not lose something in believing, as the modernists urged us to believe, that such hard-won solutions should be thrown away, so as to begin again from a state of architectural innocence (which is really a state of guilt)?

My second general consideration in favour of the vernacular arises from the first. The vernacular style, like the classical idiom from which it derives, establishes a continuity between structure and decoration. It brings to architecture our natural instinct to make a world in our own image – to imitate the proportions and features of man himself, and to transcribe into stone the symbols of our life and its joys. Its easy to-ing and fro-ing between architectural order and sculptural ornament, between formal posture and explicit representation, informs our every attempt at homebuilding. If man is to be at home in the world, then he must make the world in his own image, and – occasionally – in the image of the angel he aspires to be. In its humble way, the classical vernacular aims to transform the city into a temple, to spread over the human world the mantle of grace that is given to us in such great works of genius as Sansovino's *Loggetta* of St Mark's. Churches and temples are the places where art and architecture touch, and where life is passed from the one to the other. And the classical Orders, which begin from the sacred use of verticals, carry the gifts of art to every corner of the city.

Fig. 13 The buried column in a corner at S. Marco, Rome

ARCHITECTURE AND THE MORAL TEMPER OF THE TIMES

Richard MacCormac

Ruskin reminds us of the conditions for the aesthetic dimension of human culture to flourish.
Peter Fuller, *The Geography of Mother Nature*.

I find parts of *The Stones of Venice* deeply moving and, of course, marvellous to read. Ruskin, from what seems to me a youthful and innocent frame of mind, a spiritual Garden of Eden, calls out to our sense of wholeness, to the bright, clear, elemental, good and truthful world, which he feels architecture and the allied arts will represent.

What remains important about Ruskin, which even his opponent Geoffrey Scott allowed, was that he raised the value of architecture and reminded us – and I quote Scott – "that the arts are justified by the way they make men feel". This may be so obvious as to seem platitudinous, but architecture has served, or pretended to serve, many other purposes than art and the various nineteenth century fallacies which Scott opposed in his book *The Architecture of Humanism* remain surprisingly alive in this century. It was only twenty five years ago that a Fabian pamphlet was in circulation entitled *Architecture, Art, or Social Service*.

As a practising architect, this central meaning is immensely important to me because it seems to proclaim the integrity of architecture against the forces which oppose it – materialism, bureaucratic accountability, expedience, apathy and social conformity. Few outside the profession are aware of the extent to which architecture is determined by financial considerations and the extent to which architects are agents of this system, unequipped with some commensurate conviction which they can use in opposition. I know this because I was recently forced to resign from master-planning the redevelopment of Spitalfields, an important, historic part of London, because the developer/client wished to pursue a commercial policy which I believed to be fundamentally unsympathetic to the area.

The difficulty with Ruskin's book, particularly if you are an agnostic, as I am, is to determine the modern equivalent of his peculiarly nineteenth century moral quest and make the connection between his extraordinary rhetoric – what Yeats might have called "the will trying to do the work of the imagination" – and his examination of Venetian architecture, with its almost botanical exactitude. Ruskin raises connections between architecture and morality, architecture and nature, and architecture and the integrity of the artist, which were contentious in the nineteenth century and remain even more so today.

Ruskin followed in the steps of Pugin in giving moral significance to architectural style. Part of Geoffrey Scott's argument in *The Architecture of Humanism* is that not only is such an association irrelevant, but it actually discourages a real discourse about architecture and the obligations which architecture has to itself as an art, because it is concerned with extraneous issues. Curiously, this issue is still alive in Britain, but now the style is classicism and some of its proponents, notably Quinlan Terry and, to a lesser extent, Leon Krier, believe in its divine justification, now coupled with the magic of royal support.

Ruskin's moral position may have its origins in the distrust of architecture and the allied arts in England which followed the Reformation and the subsequent need, which is particularly English, to try to describe and justify the visual arts in terms which are substitutes for their actual intentions. Mark Girouard, in his excellent book on the great Elizabethan architect Robert Smythson, suggests that the moral temper of the Reformation in England suppressed architecture in gentlemen's education because it was Papist by association and seemed to have powers of immodesty, enchantment and extravagance associated with a profligate church and state.[1]

Of course, the aristocratic patronage of the seventeenth and eighteenth centuries restored the Italianate indulgences of architecture, and it is with the emergence of Pugin that we meet again a puritanical polemic about architecture as a moral force which Ruskin inherits. One can see that, in the English climate of ideas reacting to the burgeoning Industrial Revolution, architecture as a social art, rather than simply an aristocratic one, was seen to be insufficient in itself to oppose the new forces. The appeal to morality would shake people's conduct more than appeals to art, so architecture as an art was subsumed within a moral crusade. I think the English are still of a mind that the arts are somewhat extraneous unless some higher power tells them otherwise. Is this, I wonder, the force of H.R.H. The Prince of Wales' intervention. I think, to some extent, it is.

Ruskin wrote "We usually fall into much error by considering the intellectual powers as having dignity in themselves and separate from the heart". Nevertheless, I feel that Ruskin's form of criticism and attitude to architecture is remote from the actual implementation of the arts of which he writes. It is, perhaps, part of that presumption in British education that writing and talking about the arts has a higher status than accomplishing them. Most universities in Britain have departments of Fine Art. Fewer have departments of Architecture and in some of these architecture is concealed within Faculties of

---

1   M. Girouard, *Robert Smythson and the Architecture of the Elizabethan Era*, London, 1966.

more social and maybe moral relevance, like Sociology at the University of Edinburgh. The subject of architecture is more presentable to the university community, not as an art in itself, but subsumed within a more readily accountable academic discipline.

Without wishing to lay this entirely before Ruskin's door, or to digress too far, I think it is worth recollecting the curricula of architectural schools in the 1960s and 70s, which developed this kind of moral substitution and displaced architecture into various academic studies, planning, social science, environmental science, psychology, and occasionally aesthetics, as a carefully separate topic. The most complete course of this kind was, perhaps not surprisingly, at University College London, Jeremy Bentham's Utilitarian Foundation, where I spent two tormented years. Here the seeming inexactitude and subjectivity of architectural education was replaced with what Professor Llewellyn Davies referred to as "a new body of knowledge" which re-defined the subject. He had, indeed, re-defined architecture as a void at the centre of his curriculum – an architecture-shaped hole.

I do not intend to dwell here on the various moral poses struck by the modern movement. They have been recorded admirably in David Watkin's book *Morality and Architecture*,[2] and ludicrous much of the polemic sounds today! However, one needs to be cautious about what artists and architects say they are doing and the relationship between what they say and what they actually do, which is likely to be rather unreliable. Perhaps what occurs is analogous to Jung's theory about alchemy. The alchemists describe their works in terms of conscious material objectives. What is really going on, Jung claims, are a series of subconscious processes with their own psychological structure and objectives. David Watkins included James Stirling in his version of the ethical fallacy of modernism. His book was published in 1977, the year that Stirling won the competition for the Stadtsgallerie in Stuttgart, with a proposition which fused the neo-classicism of Schinkel with a playful sense of those original purist forms of the modern movement, the syncopated curves and unexpected collages of Ozenfant and Le Corbusier. This single building shed the moralising tone of modernism and suggested a language of architecture which could freely use history without pastiche and incorporate its immediate past in an unexpected way. It both confirmed and subverted Watkins' argument. Architecture continuously produces its own imperatives which force their way up through intellectual prescriptions like wild plants appearing through paving. Ruskin's *The Stones of Venice* barely addresses this capacity of architecture itself to move

---

2 Oxford, 1977

us, but instead sees architecture, and perhaps challenges architecture to be, the matrix of the other visual arts. For me, Ruskin does not address himself to the real force of European Gothic architecture which lies in its ever-changing expression of structural energy within highly developed and changing geometric disciplines, which infuse the whole building as a work of art. Had this been his intention, Ruskin would surely have found his gothic in France or England, instead of Venice where the influence is as much from Islam as from the north. Indeed, in one of the few analyses of structure which he introduces he attributes the cusp form of a gothic arch to the requirement of structural stiffness, whereas, in fact it is a decorative device derived from the section of an Islamic pendentive vault.

Ruskin inspired the creativity of architects such as Burgess, Butterfield and Street, each of whom, in different ways, offers polychromatic visions combining architecture with the other applied arts – something almost lost today in Britain, except perhaps in the output of John Outram. But these architects, like Gaudi in Spain, developed their own architectural language, for in his idea of gothic, Ruskin only offers an attitude which was to become an easily assumed dress, much like the appliqué classicism and post modernism of today. Ruskin eventually regretted the effect of his Venetian enthusiasms. In a letter to the *Pall Mall Gazette,* 1872, he wrote:

> I am proud enough to hope that I have had some direct influence on Mr Street. But I have [also] had indirect influence on nearly every cheap villa-builder between [Denmark Hill] and Bromley; and there is scarcely a public house near the Crystal Palace but sells its gin and bitters under pseudo-Venetian capitals copied from the Church of the Madonna of Health of Miracles. And one of my principal notions for leaving my present house [and fleeing to Brantwood in the Lake District] is that it is surrounded everywhere by the accursed Frankenstein monsters of, indirectly, my own making.

This, I suppose, is the risk taken by any historian or critic who decides to promote a style.

One nineteenth-century architect who profoundly understood and sympathised with the dilemma in Ruskin's idea was Voysey. Voysey understood the difference between the promotion of an attitude and the need of architecture to speak with its own voice and convey its own meanings. Voysey made a distinction between what he called the associative and the intrinsic in architecture, recognising that gothic, as a superficially applied style, might carry an associative connotation, but would not necessarily have intrinsic character or what he called artistic fitness. "There is all the difference", he wrote "between such associations and that inward intensity of feeling that produces an object", and he went on to consider the kinds of feelings which architecture and furniture might really evoke through their appearance, such as dignity, grace and calm. Voysey was trying to bring Ruskin's high-flying psychology of architecture down to the specific case of domestic design.

Between the idea of moral temper and the aesthetics of the physical object is human life, which tests and fulfils and, one might say, consummates the connection.

Voysey believed that good qualities could be infused into objects by design and by craftsmanship and that the objects would then convey these qualities to their users. As an architect and furniture designer, Voysey can be much more specific than Ruskin about the kinds of qualities which construction can convey. His attitude is founded in the virtues of domestic life and its expression through architecture – "the house should be the most peaceful, restful, simple servant we possess", he wrote. With other architects of the arts and crafts movement, he arrived, under the influence of Ruskin, at the quintessentially English image of domestic life which was to become universally known throughout Europe and America. *The Boston Architectural Review* in 1904 commented that "it is not too much to say that no other nation has succeeded in developing a domestic architecture having the subtle and intimate charm which in the English country house makes so strong an appeal to love of home, as well as to the love of beauty".

Voysey produced work of great beauty and serenity, in some ways reminiscent of the Shaker tradition and, not surprisingly, a number of his clients were Quakers. Here is a source of a recurring sensibility in modern domestic architecture represented too in the work of other arts and crafts architects, such as Mackintosh, which tends to be eclipsed by the purist and mechanistic arguments of European modernism. This is the sense of simplicity or perhaps one should call it "sufficiency" to give a particular moral overtone. In Voysey's work, the roofs, chimneys and traditional materials speak of a vernacular architecture which responds to essential, rather than to superfluous, needs. Wide doorways and large fireplaces express generosity. Long, horizontal runs of continuous casement windows admit light and air, suggesting an openness and easy relationship with nature, and white walls inside and out, and sparse decoration, confirm a restrained domesticity.

These inherent qualities in Voysey's architecture, also in the work of Mackintosh and Bailey Scott, were widely published in the magazine *The Studio*, influencing in turn the Swedish painter Carl Larsson. Larsson is important because he conveys an image of life conducted with aesthetic simplicity through the poetic images of his painting, which fuse the spiritual and the physical into images of happiness, often represented through records of his own family living out the events of their lives. Here is a resolution of art in life in a Ruskinian sense, although it could hardly be further from *The Stones of Venice*.

Architects tend to associate these virtues of simplicity with the noisy polemic of Le Corbusier and with his aphorisms, such as "espace, verdure, soleil" but I think that Larsson, a painter not an architect, had a wide influence, not sufficiently acknowledged today. In 1910, he published a book called *At Solsidan – On the Sunny Side* – and he went on to publish a number of books in Scandinavia and Germany which were widely read before the First World War. Larsson was a conscious propagandist, a crusader in the Ruskinian mould, illustrating his own house as the example, and it is said that no other house in the world has been as widely publicised as his.

These ideas form part of what one might call "the spiritual economy of modernism," which developed from the arts and crafts movement into the production of industrially manufactured buildings and furniture. In England the social meaning of this was highly ambiguous and continues to be so. There is the continuing sense that the elegant sufficiency represented by well-made and simple things is a reaction against the over-ripe, opulent, stifling clutter of the late nineteenth century. Fastidiousness appears as an antidote to satiety. On the other hand, perhaps this is a middle class perception and in the public sector of housing, for instance, the stripped aesthetic of Modernism carries connotations of meanness and poverty and lack of choice. For those who can choose as consumers, the context in which modern design has been acceptable has been one in which its machine-made simplicity has been combined with the plainness of old things – quarry tiled floors, Provençal cooking pots, wicker chairs and so forth – a combination which has been facetiously referred to as "conspicuous thrift".

The other inheritance of the arts and crafts movement which comes through Voysey is the sense that the significance of buildings is not just in their appearance and aesthetic, but in the quality discovered in their use, in the use of places, not spaces, and in the use of things which convey their sense of fitness in the way they are made. This is entirely distinct from architectural disciplines which impose external form on internal organisation, or largely concern themselves, as Post-Modernism does, with the spectacle, rather than the experience, of buildings. Gillian Darley and Peter Davey, in an editorial for the *Architectural Review* entitled "Sense and Sensibility", which included a discussion on our building for Worcester College, Oxford – The Sainsbury Building – wrote: "In contrast, the romantic pragmatists [this is how we were described] continue the Modern Movement or [more precisely] the Puginian Gothic Revival belief that structure should inform space, construction inform detail, and that the interior should inform the exterior – and that inside and out must be intimately related in an organic way.".

Even office buildings, we believe, are susceptible to this approach, which puts the social organisation of the building before the conventional, commercial idea that offices are a Taylorist human factory of standardised spaces. We have recently completed an office building for Hampshire County Council which, in some ways, is more like an Arts and Crafts movement country house in which the clerical work is conducted in airy, top–lit halls from which staircases ascend to landings serving clusters of individual offices. The idea of the building has been derived from an idea of how life might be conducted within it and, although the office worker is unlikely to achieve that creative personal freedom which was the birthright of Ruskin's medieval craftsmen, we have at least set the County's employees free from the enslavement of the regimented office plan, and the people who work in the building are surprised and delighted by this.

With other nineteenth century thinkers, Ruskin believed that nature was good as it showed Divine order and proved the existence of God, and just as God made nature, so, he believed, the artist and architect would, by their actions, mimic natural creation and the way in which God had gone about making things.

It is this profound sense of nature which inspires Ruskin's most deeply moving prose, for he sees, in what he calls the "Redundancy" of Gothic Architecture, the profuse and prolific energy of nature channelled through the craftsmen as "the rude love of decorative accumulation" and "magnificent enthusiasm". A poignant passage conveys Ruskin's feeling that man's work can barely match the work of nature:[3]

> ...the minute and various work of Nature made him [the craftsman] feel more forcibly the barrenness of what was best in that of man... and where he saw throughout the universe a faultless beauty lavished on measureless spaces of broidered field and blooming mountain, [he grudged] his poor and imperfect labour [until] the Cathedral front was at last lost in the tapestry of its traceries, like a rock among the thickets and herbage of spring.

---

3 *The Stones of Venice*, 2, 1853, p.208

But, in spite of this extraordinary vaulting prose, Ruskin's manner of studying architecture in Venice was like that of a student of botany, classifying his types and arranging them in rows – the orders of Venetian arches, capitals, roofs, leafage and so on – an approach to architecture which was to become commonplace in academic text books, such as Banister Fletcher's *A History of Architecture on the Comparative Method*.[4] From the types he described characteristics of style – savageness, changefulness, naturalism etc. There are beautiful descriptions and illustrations of natural and man-made forms, but no realisation that architectural organisation might itself have deep affinities with Nature. There is a chasm between the objective and the description.

The term "organic architecture", which has one of its roots in Ruskin, is now widely and loosely applied. It includes the current concern for ecological ways of building, using natural materials and energy conserving techniques. Examples are David Lea's and Richard Burton's experiments with saplings and forest thinnings, and there are a number of architects who are committed to the use of renewable building resources. At a more symbolic and abstract level, architects like Reima Pietila, working in the tradition established by Alvar Aalto, are producing work which is imitative of natural structures with the forms of plants, crystals and rock formations. There is an analogous tradition of structural design which evokes naturalistic description – petal-like, tree-like, bone-like. Gaudi developed such a language of form in Catalonia and in the last decade his kinsman, the sculptor/engineer Calatrava, has produced a range of work, including a proposal for a new bridge across the Thames, which often originates in analogies with plant or animal forms.

Ideas such as these emerged in the nineteenth century, going further than Ruskin in finding affinities between architecture and Nature, and making connections between attitude and observation which Ruskin failed to do.

Both Louis Sullivan and Frank Lloyd Wright saw the creative process itself as part of nature and architecture as part of natural law. Sullivan's terminology is highly idiosyncratic and perhaps deliberately mystifying, but in his polemic, *A System of Architectural Ornament According with a Philosophy of Man's Powers*,[5] he manages to convey an analogy between natural growth and the creative process of the artist. "Hence for the germ of the typical plant seed, with its residual power, he [the artist] may substitute, in thought, his own will as the seat of vital power in the figurative or imagined seed germ, which shall be the utterly simple energy basis of a theory of efflorescence involving plastic control over the inorganic."

---

4 First published, London, 1896
5 New York, 1924

Sullivan accompanies this wordy text with a series of extremely interesting illustrations which show the development of various patterns, some derived from stages of actual plant growth, probably taken from Asa Gray's *School and Field Book of Botany*, 1869, and others derived from geometry. In each case patterns are elaborated from simple structures, such as a square, pentagon, triangle, through a series of stages which have their own aesthetic order based on the underlying geometry. Sullivan called this process "efflorescence" and although the product sometimes has a feverish Celtic intensity, the residual structure is always there holding the thing together, like a Gothic rose window.

Wright was deeply affected by Sullivan's ideas about geometric and natural forms – "this innate or organic property of all form," he wrote, "if not merely looked at, but looked into as structure, absorbed me". The connection here, for Wright, which I have written about elsewhere, was Wright's *Froebel's Pedagogics of the Kindergarten*. Froebel, like British contemporaries such as Philip Gosse, Adam Sedgwick and Ruskin, was convinced that the natural world was God's work, and that in it could be found an "original unity" a "logic of nature" which would make the basis of an educational system through which mankind would grow in harmony with Nature itself.

"God's works reflect the logic of his spirit" wrote Froebel in the introduction to the 1877 American edition of his *Kindergarten* – "and human education cannot do anything better than imitate the logic of Nature". Frank Lloyd Wright, in an article of 1908, was to say "given inherent vision, there is no source so fertile, so suggestive, so helpful aesthetically for the architect as the comprehension of natural law".

Wright inherited a Ruskinian sense of the sanctity of Nature, but it was through Froebel and through Sullivan's confirmation of what Froebel stood for, that this sense of nature became integral with his work as an architect. Froebel was apprenticed to the crystallographer Christian Samuel Weiss [1780 – 1856], who was a founder of the science of crystallography and whose observations influenced not only the subject of crystallography itself, but theories of natural structure in general. Froebel's *Kindergarten* exercises are based on various crystalline nets or grids in which sequential transformations of symmetrical patterns can be set out. The geometries include the arrangement of squares, rectangles and diamonds, which make an increasingly complex combinations of axial and rotational symmetries, intersecting crosses and squares, pinwheels and pentagonal and hexagonal forms.

Wright's early work, particularly the Prairie Period up to 1912, shows plans, such as that of Unity Temple for example, which are directly comparable with the rectilinear cross in square patterns of the *Kindergarten*. Later, more complex forms like his unbuilt project for St Mark's Tower in the Bowery, in which squares and cruciforms are rotated in relation to each other, imitate the rotational structure of crystals and Wright seems to acknowledge this source in a development of the idea for a site in Washington which he called "Crystal Heights" – an unbuilt project of 1940.

Wright was the child of that same great sense of Nature which inspired Ruskin, but he fills out what Ruskin could not, and realises with the energy and plasticity of the great artist, the actions which lie between aspiration and observation. He wrote of his Froebel education:[6]

> The virtue of all this lay in the awakening of the child-mind to rhythmic structure in Nature – giving the child a sense of innate cause-and-effect, otherwise far beyond child comprehension. I soon became susceptible to constructive pattern *evolving in everything I saw*. I learned to "see" this way, and when I did I did not care to draw casual incidentals of Nature, I wanted to *design*.

This seeing into things went beyond the *Kindergarten* prototypes and beyond Sullivan's decorative theories. Trained to see in this way, Wright was for ever observing new analogies between Nature and structural design. The lily pond outside the Tokyo Imperial Hotel became the great clerical administration space in the Johnson Wax Building in Racine, the stems and pads of the lilies becoming the columns and capitals, the tubular glass spanning between the effect of the surface shimmer of water above. The helical structures of plants and shells became the Guggenheim Museum. At Falling Water, the great rocky outcrop of the site itself seems to be extended and cantilevered as a building which floats amongst the trees.

The society which Ruskin sought and which he felt to be the necessary condition for art and architecture in his chapter entitled "Gothic Architecture", did not come about and it remains as it was conceived – an imaginary ideal with which to continue to judge the conduct and the products of industrial society.

But, in his conclusion, Ruskin also describes the necessary temper of the artist himself, the inner integrity of his actions and the function of art "to rouse the imagination from its palsy" and he goes on to make his celebrated attack on classicism: "an architecture intended as it seems, to make plagiarists of its architects, slaves of its workmen..." This text is a reminder of the integrity of

---

6 *Frank Lloyd Wright: Wright: Writings and Buildings,* Selected by E. Kaufmann and B. Raeburn, Meridian Books, New York, 1960, p.19.

the artist's or architect's own thought, and of the danger of succumbing to conventions and superficial uses of style which substitute for real architectural thought. Once again in Britain the convention of classicism is being used in commercial architecture. Its authenticity as an architectural language is atrophied by inappropriate scale and structure. But it satisfies a certain kind of social approval, what Ruskin called "the dim eyed proprieties of the multitude".

The very difficult question in Europe, particularly in Britain where we hang on to our cities as a physical memory of our past, which we try to preserve and confirm, is the place of inventive new architecture and the extent to which it should be constrained in manner by the situation in which it is built. Much of my own practice's work is in historically sensitive sites in Oxford and Cambridge. Although we feel constrained, to some extent, by traditional materials, scale and form, we avoid imitation and pastiche and seek a relationship with the context through what I call a narrative.

Our best known building in Oxford, the Sainsbury Building, looks nothing like the early eighteenth century buildings which form the College quadrangle, but offers a similar sequence of experiences, which are reactions to places, rather than to elevations. The old buildings form a threshold between the College and the City. The threshold itself is a loggia under the library, and once you enter the loggia you become aware of the magic park in the College grounds, and as you progress beyond, you find what has hitherto not been revealed, a serpentine lake. This unfolding sequence is discovered in our own building, which also forms the threshold between College and city and stands at the other end of the lake, opposite the original quadrangle. These ideas derive, to some extent, from eighteenth century landscape theory, but need no support from the superficial imitation of architectural style.

We live in a period, in Britain, of architectural ingratiation, which I think Ruskin would have despised. Post-Modernism has encouraged a kind of over-talkative conversational architecture which tries to be polite to everything around it, but usually lacks any inherent conviction of its own.

We confuse the appearance of architecture with its spirit, as the criteria for approval, particularly in the area of planning legislation, become increasingly mundane and trivial. I can hardly imagine a great architect like the late Louis Kahn getting a building accepted in England today. I have often ruminated over what would have happened if he had lived to be able to make a submission for the extension to the National Gallery in Trafalgar Square. He did not know how to ingratiate himself or how to play the dextrous contextual games of his best known pupil, and perhaps the best known betrayer of his principles, Robert Venturi. The Yale Museum, which houses the Mellon Collection of British Art is not pretty, nor is his library for St Phillip's Academy in Exeter, New Hampshire. Both are noble works by an evidently noble and spiritual man, a Ruskinian affirmation!

Architecture remains a moral adventure and I believe it has to keep transforming tradition to re-awaken meanings, rather than imitate old forms. I feel this personally, having recently been refused planning permission for a new Chapel for a school in the south-east of England. The proposed building accommodates a congregation in a great timber structure like an ark, comparable with the idea of a gothic choir separately contained within the larger masonry envelope of the church and roofed with a ribbed structure of timber and stainless steel, derived from various sources, including the late Gothic Divinity School in the Bodleian Library. The opposition want either a restoration of the burned out Edwardian Gothic Chapel, or an imitation-Gothic building. For me, the choice is between imitation and the spirit of the idea. I wonder whether Ruskin would be on my side!

PLACE AND MOMENT: THE EMERGENCE OF A PUBLIC ARCHITECTURE

Norman Hammond

Public architecture is the product of, and the setting for, public life: such a life is only perceived to exist when a society has attained sufficient complexity that actions can be divided between the public and private spheres. While even the architecture of private life has its public face, as Glazer and Lilla note[1], I do not propose to explore the subtleties of that interface today. I am concerned, instead, with when and why public architecture comes into existence, and whether a case can be made for its development as a necessary concomitant of complex society.

The public architecture of our Western tradition, the Classical-Gothic-Renaissance-Revival-Modern continuum, has a history of some 2500 years, one that is largely familiar to us all, a framework within which the polemics of architectural critics and the debates of historians flourish. That there was a public architecture before the emergence of the Greek styles is something that has concerned scholars only for the past two centuries: while the Great Pyramid was drawn in admirable cross-section as early as 1638, the halls of Karnak at Luxor had to await the arrival of Napoleon's savants to attain fame, and the lost cities of Assyria and Sumer, the attentions of men such as Austen Layard in the middle of the nineteenth century. The ancestral architecture of Bronze Age Greece and Crete was exposed only towards the end of the century, when Heinrich Schliemann went hunting for the reality behind Homer, and into the present age with Sir Arthur Evan's excavation of the Minotaur's lair at Knossos. The Minoans of Crete, like the Hittites of central Anatolia and the earliest civilisation of Mesopotamia, were a people known only from elliptical references in Egyptian texts until the archaeologist's spade brought them to light. Their influence on the development of the Western tradition in public architecture is difficult to evaluate: the Greek Dark Age between 1000 and 700 B.C. has yet to yield convincing ancestors for the temples of the Archaic and Classical periods, but the Mycenaean megaron with its antechamber and main room, and the heroön of Lefkandi on Euboea have been seen as links between the architecture of the prehistoric and the historic world.

Certainly, one of the things that strikes us when we study the public architecture of such early civilisations is how often we can confidently apply functional

---

1 Nathan Glazer and Mark Lilla, *The Public Face of Architecture,* New York, 1987, p. ix.

labels to buildings on the basis of plan and elevation: the Palace of Minos at Knossos, with its ranks of storerooms, throne room, and splendid courtyard, could be seen as the seat of a ruler and his administration long before Michael Ventris deciphered Linear B and allowed the detail of Mycenaean tribute and workshop economy to be elucidated. The ziggurats of Sumer and Akkad were interpreted correctly as the high places of the gods before the reading of cuneiform texts allowed us to name them as Enlil or Nanna, or to identify their builders. The architecture of religion and government in complex societies has for millennia had characteristics which render it instantly recognisable: it is, perhaps, among the problems that today's public architecture faces, that the archaeologist of the future could not be so certain.

While it is not my aim today to summarise the history of public architecture in the ancient Old World, let me set up a chronological yardstick against which we can measure the New World which I shall discuss: until the end of the Ice Age, just over 10,000 years ago, humans were seasonally mobile gatherers, fishers and hunters. Where there were caves or rock shelters, they used them as dwellings, and in parts of Europe, Africa, and Australia decorated them with powerful symbols. Here in Australia we are fortunate in having continuity of culture, so that some of the meaning of the Dreamtime can be explicated; the same goes for the art of the San in southern Africa, and ideas gleaned from these two continents are now being applied to the Stone Age art of Europe, which goes back some 30,000 years.

When early humans left the shelter of the rocks, they constructed dwellings from perishable materials: the earliest human construction known is a windbreak of boulders and branches at Olduvai Gorge in Tanzania that goes back some 1.75 million years. Of such shelters only the footings or postholes survive: most were occupied for a few months at most, and what is amazing is that any evidence of them survives at all. Longer-term dwellings accompanied the economic transformation which took place in several areas of the globe around the end of the Ice Age, what the great Australian prehistorian Gordon Childe termed "the Neolithic Revolution". While the deep causes of this process are still hotly debated, what happened is clear: from about 9000 B.C. onwards wheat and barley were brought into domestication, together with sheep and goats, followed swiftly by other cereals and by cattle and pigs. The successful management of this economic package demanded sedentary occupation in the same place year-round, although the first villagers seem to have been harvesting and sowing wild cereals for a few generations before visible domestication occurred. The storage of produce and the penning of stock created a need for permanent buildings, what Ruskin called "the Architecture of Protection", intended to shelter "men or their possessions from violence of any kind, whether of men or of the elements". Ruskin included hut and sheepfold, palace and fortress, within this category and made the important point that amenity, "commodiousness and comfort of habitation", was an integral part of protective architecture.

Investment in fields and crops, stock and housing, needed active protection from early on: the walls of Jericho were first raised to defend the village there and its perennial spring more than ten millennia ago. The walls were of coursed rubble, and included a solid drumlike tower standing some eight metres (26 feet) high, pierced by a narrow stair passage. Here we have the earliest public, in the sense of non-domestic, architecture in the world, a testament to the existence of cupidity and aggression even in the world of the first farmers.

Within 2,000 years the agricultural economy and village life had spread all across the Middle East from Pakistan to Greece: hundreds of ancient settlements are known, of which one of the best-documented is Çatal Hüyük in the Konya plain of southern Turkey. Here by 8500 years ago there was a town, covering 32 acres (13 ha) and with a population estimated at several thousand. The buildings were agglomerated, their entries through the roofs. While from outside they all looked the same, a number of the unicellular structures were not houses but shrines, decorated with the skulls of bulls and goats and with plaster reliefs of felines. We have here the appearance of religious function in building, but within the structural format of the dwelling house (reminding us, perhaps, of the house-churches of early Christendom): temples built as the visible and explicit homes of the gods did not appear for several centuries.

The earliest of these is at Eridu, in southern Mesopotamia, a single small room 4.5 by 3.5 metres (16 by 12 feet) with a central pedestal and an "altar" facing the entry, dating to around 5400 B.C. It is the first of seventeen superimposed temples, progressively larger, higher, and more imposing, that Seton Lloyd excavated in the 1930s, and documents the emergence of the ziggurat or high place. By 4500 B.C. these temples, of mudbrick on platforms of clay or imported stone and reached by a stair, had façades decorated with projections and recesses, and later with mosaics of coloured cones and bitumen: the form and the decoration of these structures proclaimed their function.

The emergence of public architecture, in most cultures monumental brick or masonry construction, out of a background of private shelter construction, and its relationship to urbanism, political structure, and the role of élites, has been a focus of enquiry in Old World archaeology longer than in prehispanic America, but in the latter area it is now a burgeoning field of research, and one approached within the anthropological rather than historical tradition. Stanley Loten notes that "we currently operate with a largely unquestioned and possibly somewhat unconsciously assumed model, that monumentality is essentially epiphenomenal with respect to dynamics of culture" and are inclined to assume that "expanded access to labor and goods was celebrated in the construction of massive centres, an assumption leading to the further assumption that as élites increased their power they "developed access to more resources and began to erect huge structures celebrating hierarchical authority through cosmic sanction'"[2]. This model assumes that monumental architecture "primarily reflects expressions of wealth and power already acquired, rather than something of general societal value for establishing authority and maintaining social order". Loten believes that the converse is true, at least for the Preclassic Maya: that "an emerging élite grasped the value of monumental architecture during the Late Preclassic [400 B.C.–A.D. 250] and began building impressive temples and shrines to increase the self-evident nature of their own and their descendants' claim to supernatural kinship, thereby securing their right and access to power: they did not do this merely or even primarily as conspicuous display or celebration".

I shall return to the Maya as a case study in Pre-Columbian public architectural development in a moment, but before I do, there are some basic facts about the New World cultural tradition that we must carry in the forefront of our minds.

The first point is that it is an autonomous tradition, a development of civilisation totally independent of the parallel process in the Old World. The Amerindians crossed into their new world – not that they knew it to be such – at some point late in the Pleistocene Ice Age, when lower sea levels worldwide had exposed a land bridge between Siberia and Alaska some 900 miles wide. The date of this penetration is still a matter of active and vocal scholarly dispute, with the conservatives arguing for about 12,000 years ago, the moderates for around 20,000 and the radicals for 30,000 upwards. This is not unlike the argument over the first settlement of Australia, now resolved in favour of the radicals by Rhys Jones's new dates from Malakunanja II in the Northern Territory, of over 50,000 years ago. There is, however, total agreement that the first Americans arrived as gathers and hunters before the end of the Ice Age, and thousands of years before the beginning of farming.

American agriculture is also autochthonous: where the cultures of Eurasia cultivated wheat, barley, oats and rye, the native Americans created maize by the domestication of teosinte; where the Old World had a range of domestic

---

2 Review of J.C. Gerhardt, *Preclassic Maya Architecture at Cuello, Belize, Journal of Field Archaeology*, 17, 1990, p. 493

animals for meat, milk, wool, hides and traction, the New World had only the dog, in Mexico the turkey, and in Peru the guinea pig, llama and alpaca. Of these species only the dog, which may well have accompanied the Ice Age hunters, is also found in Asia. The consequence of this disparity is that animal products played a much smaller part in the Pre-Columbian economy, and the bulk of those were the primary products of flesh and hides. The secondary products obtained by keeping rather than killing animals (such as milk and its derivatives – cheese, yogurt, etc.) were either absent or developed in only a limited area, such as the woollen textiles and carrying capacity obtained from the llama and alpaca of the central Andes. The lack of any larger animal for traction meant that the wheel, although invented in principle (wheeled toys are known from Mexico and El Salvador dating to ca. A.D. 600-900), had no application in practice: human muscle power was the motive force in the creation of New World civilisation.

Another distinction from the civilisations of Eurasia and Africa is the late development of metallurgy, and the minor extent to which metal was used even then for anything except ornaments. Gold, silver, platinum and copper-working were developed in the northern Andes in the first millennium B.C., at least 3,000 years later than the first metalworking in the Old World. Iron was already being used in western Asia before the first gold was beaten or poured in Peru. The new technology spread slowly northwards, but did not reach Mexico or the Maya area until civilisation was well established. The Aztec warriors who fought Cortes used swords edged with obsidian, although they wore jewellery of copper and sometimes gold: the Spanish conquest destroyed a culture on the brink of the Bronze Age.

This paucity of the economic resources which we accept as part of the necessary infrastructure of the complex societies of the Middle East, the Mediterranean, and the oriental civilisations of India, Southeast Asia and China, makes the American achievement the more striking: the great temples of Maya Tikal and Aztec Tenochtitlan and the masonry of Inca Cuzco were created by people with a technological base poorer than that of the builders of Stonehenge.

This autonomy of New World civilisation has been apparent since the work of Franz Kugler[3] and John Lloyd Stephens[4] demonstrated the self-contained character of its architectural and artistic traditions, and that resemblances to the arts of other regions such as India or Egypt were best explained as convergences rather than borrowings. Nevertheless, the possibility of diffusion of developed

---

3 *Handbuch der Kunstgeschichte,* Stuttgart 1842
4 *Incidents of Travel in Central America, Chiapas and Yucatan,* New York 1841

cultural traits by seaborne voyages has been raised within the last half century by Thor Heyerdahl, and most recently and cogently for transpacific contacts with China by Joseph Needham and Lu Gwei-djen.[5] Even the latter, though, admit "that nothing in [their] review detracts from the formidable originality of the Amerindian cultures...the great artistic and liturgical sensibility of the Meso-American peoples... their great achievements in architecture, especially the planning of ceremonial centres, and to a lesser extent in hydraulic engineering". George Kubler notes that the diffusionists argue for transmission of symbolic aspects of culture, but not for utilitarian ones, although the latter are the most effectively transmitted in documented instances of interregional diffusion; he shows that all of the features proposed as Asian stimuli to American culture were themselves only particular expressions of ideas found across the whole of Eurasia, and did not stem from any "focus". The parallels are accidental arrivals at the same destination from different directions: if any do have a common origin it lies deep in the Ice Age.

The question of Amerindian independence is an important one for Old World culture historians, as Kubler notes: "The linked sequences of Old World history afford no opportunity to verify the thesis of distinct cultural traditions arising from independent origins. Only America provides the possibility of establishing a case for independent invention".[6]

In architecture the parallels include the construction of dwellings with many rectangular rooms, decorated with murals, and with attached gardens stocked with cultivated fruits and flowers, sometimes with fountains or other water-works, as Jacquetta Hawkes notes.[7] These houses are clustered into cities dominated by the monumental architecture of great royal and religious buildings – divine kings in their palaces, and temples for the gods built on artificial mountains or "high places", furnished with altars for sacrificial offerings. The secular and sacred hierarchies (which may well be fused) are served by, and partly formed of, an intellectual élite concerned with the esoteric use of hieroglyphic writing, with astronomy, with mathematics and the calculation of solar, lunar and planetary calendars.

"There are conspicuous and significant differences between the first civilisations of the Old and New Worlds, but there are also very powerful and fundamental similarities," Hawkes says. "When we turn to the civilisations of the Americas and their many common features with those of the Old World we can recognise a fact of profound significance for any understanding of the creative psyche of

---

5   *Trans-Pacific Echoes and Resonances, Listening Once Again,* Singapore 1985
6   *The Art and Architecture of Ancient America,* London 1962, p. 11
7   *Nothing but or something more,* Seattle 1972, pp. 24-26

mankind, emphasised by their creation (especially the Maya) in natural environments that could hardly be more completely unlike those offered by the Tigris-Euphrates and Nile valleys." Describing the first meeting of the two worlds when Cortes came to the Aztec capital of Tenochtitlan, and the amazement of the Spaniards at the quality, but not the existence or nature, of Mesoamerican culture, she asks: "Is it not immensely telling that the representatives of two civilisations created in their worlds apart should meet so easily, find one another's manners, possessions, customs and general ideas so little different?"

Hawkes notes the technical differences, such as the absence of draught animals, wheeled vehicles, and metal tools, and points out that it is in precisely these realms of response to environmental stimuli and economic needs that cultural convergence is most to be expected even in independent societies; she thus challenges Grahame Clark's thesis that "the main drift of evolution in the sphere of economics has been towards obtaining the maximum return from the minimum expenditure of effort", offering instead the observation that the Pyramids of Egypt were not economically cost-effective and that their builders, as well as the Sumerians and later the Mesoamericans, "with any economic natural selection should surely have been eliminated".

What Hawkes is presenting in this somewhat essentialist set of observations is the notion that there are innate human characteristics which will manifest themselves in similar ways in societies that climb towards complexity. Is this so absurd? The Pre-Columbian tradition is one so foreign to our understanding, one not at the source of any of our traditions, nor nourished by any of the streams which have flowed into those traditions, that our gut reaction may be that it is absurd; the disjunction of form and meaning between the prehispanic and colonial periods is so great; but what does the Pre-Columbian archaeological and architectural record tell us? When we look at the forms of its buildings, at the problems apparently posed and the solutions reached, we find that things are less unfamiliar, less bizarre, than we might expect from a cultural tradition separated from our own since the Ice Age.

Hannah Arendt argued (in *The Public Realm: The Common*) that the public world was a shared one, intended to be transgenerational: this is precisely the attitude we can now discern in the recent decipherment of Maya monuments, recording the genealogies and deeds of their kings within a time frame of cosmic length. We could argue for its presence in one of the most common and striking features of prehispanic architecture in Mesoamerica, the cumulative piling of one building on another, the precursor deconsecrated to be used as the heart of its successor. Detailed studies of construction techniques show parallel and simultaneous tasks being carried out: the massive acropolis at the early Maya site of Nohmul in Belize was constructed by numerous gangs of workmen streaming in from different quarries and marl pits, bringing stone of slightly different colours to be stacked in modular units. The presence of plazas at the hearts of all prehispanic cities, bounded by structures communal in their scale even if of undocumented function, argue for a gathering of the populace like that remarked by Glazer and Lilla for the late medieval and Renaissance apogee of the public space, incidentally and perhaps not coincidentally the period when notions of public versus private life and places are most strongly marked in the post-Roman world. What is rare in the Pre-Columbian world is the street: away from the plaza, community plans tend to turn into clusters of compounds, on ethnographic evidence likely to be those of clans of related extended families: the movement from a kin-based to a class-based society occurred both late and sporadically in ancient America. Streets occur most frequently in communities that were imposed on the landscape, where a higher than usual degree of proximity and concentration was visited on the population in the interests of centralisation and control: Inca Cuzco and Aztec Tenochtitlan, the two last great metropoleis of the Pre-Columbian world, had street plans that were not unfamiliar to the Spanish conquistadors, while fifteen centuries earlier Teotihuacan, the first planned city in the New World, used a cruciform grid as the basis for a concentrated population stripped from the surrounding valleys.

Roger Scruton's essay in *The Public Face of Architecture* emphasises the "good manners" of the Classical styles, which I take to include a clear hierarchy of meaning, with the most emphasis on the most important structural features, with decoration enough to proclaim special functions and investment beyond that dictated by need, but restrained enough not to overwhelm the form of the building. George Kubler warns that "an architecture to which the column is an occasional relief in the rhythm of voids and solids cannot be contained by regulations derived from Vitruvius and Vignola": can we, taking this caveat, see equally good manners in the buildings of Pre-Columbian America? I believe that we can, in buildings as far apart in time and distance as the Classic Maya élite residences of Palenque and Uxmal, the temples of Tikal and Chichen Itz, and the streets and defences of Inca Cuzco.

Where we have a problem is in determining what the etiquette behind those manners is: Victor Hugo's Claude Frollo, Archdeacon of Notre-Dame, could "read" his cathedral and its surroundings as one might a hieroglyphic manu-script, the hidden meaning of the built scripture revealed slowly to the attentive "reader" while being only obscurely apparent to the casual observer;[8] but the

Archdeacon knew his text, the biblical and cultural matrix within which the cathedral had been created. When we approach the buildings of Mexico or Peru we do so without a text in hand, for as Kubler says "we cannot reconstruct any web of events without written records..artistic identities are remote and unclear... only their works tell us about them". The reconstruction of American prehistory over the past century has until very recently been unaccompanied by any knowledge of historical events. The current rapid decipherment of Maya hieroglyphic writing is giving us for the first time a detailed vision of how a prehispanic Native American people thought, and what information they felt it worth immortalising in lapidary inscriptions. The results are quite enlightening: we find that both vase painters and sculptors signed their work, and that the latter sometimes worked in teams on a complex stela, while the former included members of royal lineages. We find also that both stelae and buildings were named, the former being dubbed *te-tun* – "stone tree", with an individual sobriquet for each monument, while the latter bore such designations as "house of the mat" (a woven mat being the symbol of regal authority equivalent to "throne" in our perception) or "house of counsel", apparently where the ruler and his advisors met in conclave. What we still lack, however, and will probably always have to work without, are the motivations behind Pre-Columbian buildings. In a few instances we can make a good guess: the Palace at Palenque, for instance, an agglomerated group of single structures finding themselves eventually around courtyards. Each major range seems to have been built by an incoming ruler as his formal "seat", perhaps physically as his throne room; each building in turn seems to have been retired and turned to some other purpose after the ruler's death. The founder of Palenque's seventh century prosperity, a man called Pacal (reigned A.D. 615-683), had a funerary temple built for himself, with a stairway winding down through the pyramid to a subterranean vault where his elaborate sarcophagus awaited him, empty. Here we have buildings as symbols of identity and authority. At Teotihuacan, in central Mexico, we have a planned city with a population of between 125,000 and 200,000 people, which was imposed on the landscape in the first century A.D. and flourished for over half a millennium. The architecture of Teotihuacan, like its ground plan, is uniform in style, each block of apartments presenting a similar face to the outside, each temple offering the same slope-and-panel profile. The city, like Washington, Brasilia, and Canberra, is not an organic development but a disembedded capital, the product of dirigisme on a scale both grand and

8   Joseph Rykwert, "The Purpose of Ceremonies", *Lotus* 17, 1982

rather rare in prehispanic America. Robert Redfield and Milton Singer[9] class these modern examples as "cities of the new bureaucracies", in contrast with the managerial-entrepreneurial "cities of the main street of the world": while they do not recognise such an urban type in the preindustrial world (their division is between "administrative-cultural cities" and "cities of native commerce", Beijing and Kyoto being examples of the former and Bruges and Marseilles of the latter), Teotihuacan is *sui generis,* and some extraordinary explanation must be sought for its creation, an explanation made the more difficult by its anonymity, not only in lacking monumental texts and any other form of decipherable signs, but in its equal lack of evidence for rulership and hierarchy. Apart from one rich early burial found this year at the heart of the Ciudadela pyramid, accompanied by numerous sacrificed warriors, Teotihuacan seems acephalous: but the establishment and management of such a metropolis for half a millennium certainly required governmental organs of complex tenacity. They simply do not seem to have felt the need to make any public demonstration of their power.

There are other motives for public architecture which are equally difficult to detect without documentary evidence: we know that many of the grand buildings in Roman cities were the result of euergetism, private munificence for the public benefit, with *gloria* the only reciprocation for the outlay. As Paul Veyne points out, euergetism is by definition politically and economically irrational, exceeding whatever investment is needed to maintain personal rank or mark class stratification.[10] The practice has, to my mind, strong parallels with the potlatching practised in historic times on the Pacific coast of Canada, a form of economic levelling which is also seen in the enforced adoption of expensive ritual offices in other societies. If this was the hidden agenda of Roman euergetism it has remained well-concealed. In the case of Pre-Columbian America the practice itself, and the construction of buildings by individuals as a levelling mechanism, or for marking social layering, or to satisfy some public demand as Nero's "bread and circuses" were held to do, are all equally undetectable from the architectural and archaeological evidence.

The anonymity of Pre-Columbian architecture is its greatest drawback to those of us concerned with reconstructing how the cities and the civilisations of ancient America functioned: but the mere existence of those cities and their monumental buildings, evolved in isolation from any Old World influences, shows us that human societies will, given the necessary stimuli of adequate population size

---

9 "The Cultural Role of Cities", *Economic Development and Cultural Change* 3, 1954, pp. 53-73,
10 *A History of Private Life,* 1, pp. 107-110

and density and a sufficient technical and resource base, develop a public architecture which in its use of mass, space, decorative repertoire and regional distinctiveness is exciting, informative, and intriguing. George Canning said in 1826 that he had "called the New World into existence to redress the balance of the Old": I hope that I have tonight called the New World in evidence to show that the public architecture of the Old World should have no monopoly on our attention, and that the anonymous past presents problems as fascinating as those of the well-documented present.

ARCHITECTURE IN THE PUBLIC REALM

Dell Upton

I begin, in Australia of all places, with a prison: the State Penitentiary for the Eastern District of Pennsylvania. Authorised in 1821 and constructed at Philadelphia over the next decade and a half, Eastern State Penitentiary was the fruit of nearly a century of Euro-American debate over the nature of crime and punishment. It confined each prisoner to a single small cell in which he ate, slept, and worked throughout his sentence, without contact (in theory, at least) with any human being other than his jailer. Although these penal methods had been proposed in Britain as early as the 1770s, the Pennsylvanians were the first to try the "separate" system, as it was called. The prison attracted visitors ranging from Charles Dickens to Alexis de Tocqueville (who came to the United States to inspect it) and inspired a worldwide wave of penitentiary-building that did not subside for nearly a hundred years. Its offspring could be found from Pentonville to Port Arthur.[1]

The penitentiary resembles an octopus missing one of its arms.[2] Seven cellblocks of one or two storeys radiated from a central rotunda that served as a command point. Each arm contained a corridor lined on both sides with 12-by-8-foot cells. Eastern State's architect, John Haviland, took pains to point out that this was not a Panopticon, for in Jeremy Bentham's scheme the cells lined the perimeter of a concentric arrangement. Moreover, literal visual inspection in the Panopticon was replaced at Philadelphia by aural inspection: the vaulted corridors of the cellblocks would transmit any illicit sounds to the guards at the centre.

The cellular plan was only the chassis of this reformative machine. Haviland emphasised that "the leading feature of the System . . . depends almost entirely, on the construction of [the convict's] cell", and indeed the cells were obsessive exercises in sensory deprivation.[3] The entering prisoner travelled hooded to his cell so that he had no idea where he was located in the complex. The thickness and composition of the walls, the form of the vaulting, even the water level in the plumbing were calculated to prevent the transmission of sounds from prisoner to prisoner. Each cell was dimly illuminated by a diffusing lens set at

1   U. R. Q. Henriques, "The Rise and Decline of the Separate System of Prison Discipline", *Past and Present 54* (1972), pp. 61-93; Robert Hughes, *The Fatal Shore: The Epic of Australia's Founding,* New York, 1986, p. 550.
2   The following architectural description is taken from John Haviland's own *A Description of Haviland's Design for the New Penitentiary, Now Erecting Near Philadelphia,* Philadelphia, 1824 and from inspection of the surviving building.
3   John Haviland, letter to I. Louis Tellkampf, Oct. 11, 1842, in John Haviland papers, University of Pennsylvania, 6:94.

an angle in the ceiling vault. This permitted the entry of light but made even clouds and passing birds unrecognisable. Food was passed through the wall on a sliding tray with vertical metal sheets fastened at either end to prevent the prisoner's peeking through the slot. According to one official, the new convict heard "an address . . . by one of the functionaries of the institution, in which the consequences of his crime are portrayed, the design to be effected by his punishment manifested, and the rules of the prison, as regards the convicts amply delineated". He was "then locked up and left to the salutary admonition of a reproving conscience [without even the proverbial Bible], and the reflections which solitude usually produce[s]. . . In about two weeks, they begin to feel the horrors of solitude unemployed. . . Ennui seizes them, every hour is irksome, and they supplicate for the means of employment of the most abject humility".[4]

The penitentiary's architecture had negative and positive goals. It was designed to thwart criminal conspiracy, to promote introspection, and to produce a conscientious, obedient, hard-working manual or craft laborer. The building carried the burden of this task. A supporter of the separate system observed that this architecture "takes away the power of combination; it opposes its walls and grates to the attempts of the convict to escape. These walls and bars restrain, but do not irritate by seeming to watch and suspect him. He does not personify them, and make them objects of ill-will and hatred. His keepers . . . are less liable to be regarded with ill-will on that account".[5]

If planning enforced moral reform, appearance celebrated it. Dressed in its Gothic walls, Eastern State was "calculated to convey to our citizens the external appearance of those magnificent and picturesque castles of the middle age, which contribute so eminently to embellish the scenery of Europe". But it also had the serious task of "impart[ing] a grave, severe, and awful character to the external aspects of this building. The effect which it produces on the imagination of every passing spectator, is peculiarly impressive, solemn, and instructive".[6]

Cut to 1987. What was to be done with the penitentiary, which had been unused for nearly twenty years, except for brief service as a setting for the car-burning

---

4 [Thomas B. McElwee], *A Concise History of the Eastern Penitentiary of Pennsylvania . . . by a Member of the Legislature* Philadelphia, 1835, pp. 13-14.
5 S.G. Howe, *An Essay on the Separate and Congregate Systems of Prison Discipline;* Being a Report Made to the Boston Prison Discipline Society, Boston, 1946, p. 21.
6 McElwee, *Concise History*, p. 7. The middle generation of prisons between the old-style prisons of the mid-eighteenth century and the new-model penitentiaries relied even more heavily on visual appearance to enforce their message. See John Bender, *Imagining the Penitentiary, Fiction and the Architecture of Mind in Eighteenth-Century England,* Chicago, 1987, pp. 21, 205-6; Anthony Vidler, *The Writing of the Walls: Architectural Theory in the Late Enlightenment,* Princeton, 1987.

scene in a Mad Max movie? Originally built at the edge of the city, it was quickly engulfed by a middle-class suburb that by the 1960s had become an economically marginal Black and Hispanic neighbourhood. By the mid-eighties, the numbers of these residents were nearly equalled by the inescapable gentrifiers. The city of Philadelphia decided to turn over the derelict prison, described by the director of the city's Redevelopment Authority as "the largest undeveloped tract of land in or near Center City," to private developers.[7] All the proposals involved breaching the walls, demolishing all or most of the interior structures, and inserting parking, shopping, and services.[8] At the last moment, some Philadelphians demanded the penitentiary's preservation. On the day a contract was to be awarded to the KODE Corporation, Mayor Wilson Goode postponed any action indefinitely, pending further study of the site.[9]

In the months following, debate in the newspapers intensified when the penitentiary was opened for visitation by Philadelphians, including many lifelong neighbours who had never been inside.[10] Reacting to its physical similarity to a shopping arcade, some visitors suggested using the building as a galleria and even a souk. Others saw it as a potential homeless shelter or as a storage facility for the city's museums.[11] Proponents of development stressed the jobs and economic prosperity that would ostensibly be brought to the neighbourhood.[12] Opponents of preservation saw the building as a monument to oppression and demanded its replacement by a "peace park or an institute where people can study the issue of crime and punishment".[13] Preservationists cited the penitentiary's worldwide influence and its depiction of the social ideals of the early republic as cause for saving it.[14] Both sides pointed to the horrible failure of good intentions as support for their positions.[15] Nothing has yet been done.

The role of architecture in the public realm, and particularly its capacity for embodying and promoting civic and humane values, the subject of our

7 Vernon Loeb, "Three Bids Submitted for Penitentiary Site", *Philadelphia Inquirer,* Nov. 6, 1987, p. 7B.

8 Thomas Hine, "How to Avoid Present Fiascoes When Developing Eastern State", *Philadelphia Inquirer,* Nov. 22, 1987, p. 15-H; Margaret O. Kirk, "Wrangling on Re-Use for Prison", *New York Times,* June 12, 1988, p. 5.

9 Thomas Turcol, "Panel Reconsiders Prison Development", *Philadelphia Inquirer,* Apr. 19, 1988, p. B-1.

10 Edward Moran, "Neighbors Visit Pen", *Philadelphia Daily News,* Oct. 16, 1989, p. 6.

11 Howard Goodman, "Preservation Experts Say Old Penitentiary Should Get a New Life", *Philadelphia Inquirer,* Oct. 14, 1989, p. 1-B; Moran, "Neighbors", p. 6. The notion of the penitentiary as souk was suggested to me by the Director of City Property on a visit to the site on June 12, 1987.

12 Thomas Turcol, "Goode Scuttles Conversion of Eastern Pen", *Philadelphia Inquirer,* Apr. 30, 1988, pp. B1, B4; Abbe F. Fletman, letter to the editor, *Philadelphia Inquirer,* June 1, 1988.

13 Lois G. Forer, letter to the editor, *Philadelphia Inquirer,* July 24, 1988; Goodman, "Preservation Experts", p. 1-B.

14 Moran, *"Neighbors",* p. 6.

15 Forer, letter to the editor; Gretchen Worden, letter to the editor, *Philadelphia Inquirer,* Aug. 2, 1988; Martin Kevin Cusack, letter to the editor, *Philadelphia Inquirer,* Aug. 8, 1988.

Conversazione, is currently a hot topic in architectural and public policy circles.[16] Most of this literature has the tone of a jeremiad. The public landscape has deteriorated: once we knew what our common values were; once we confidently built magnificent public architecture that expressed them; once we built, period. These lamentations remind me of the pastoral poetry that Raymond Williams studied: in the civic, as in literature, each generation imagines a golden age just over the last hill.[17]

But the issue transcends simple nostalgia. The thesis of decline rests on a number of assumptions about the relationships among architecture, ideas, and public action; about the civic values we choose to celebrate; and about who should decide these questions. When the claim is advanced, on the one hand, that we need a public architecture that will command general assent and, on the other, that private constructions are unavoidably public and ought, therefore, to be governed by some similar sense of shared public values, we recognise the true prize sought in the debate as nothing less than the custodianship of cultural and political authority in our society.[18] Thus I introduce my discussion of the civic with this lengthy tale of a penitentiary not only from perversity, but because Eastern State's ancient and modern history embodies most of the important issues in this discussion. A historical, rather than a purely theoretical, tack is best to take if we wish to understand the roots of our current ambivalence and the possibilities for change, so I will draw on the story of the penitentiary and on the history of urban public building in general, particularly that of the city I know best, Philadelphia.

In *The Stones of Venice,* John Ruskin develops a long argument for the interdependence of architecture and morality. Ruskin claimed that the highest value of architecture was to be found less in its purity of form than in the investment of human imagination in it. Somehow, however crude the execution, the effort shines through and moves us. The artifact connects the spirit of one human being to that of another. In so arguing, Ruskin tapped into a long-lived western tradition. Westerners since the middle ages have shared a deep, often unarticulated, but profoundly materialistic belief in the connection between the outer and inner worlds. The metaphorical transitivity of our language seals the

16 For example, Rob Krier, *Urban Space,* New York, 1979; Aldo Rossi, *The Architecture of the City,* rev. ed.; Cambridge: 1982; Nathan Glazer and Mark Lilla, *The Public Face of Architecture: Civic Culture and Public Spaces,* New York, 1987; Leon Krier, "Choosing Chaos or Harmony", in *Real Architecture,* ed. Alan Powers, London, 1987, pp. 13-17; Charles T. Goodsell, *The Social Meaning of Civic Space: Studying Political Authority Through Architecture,* Lawrence, 1988; Wayne Attoe and Donn Logan, *American Urban Architecture: Catalysts in the Design of Cities,* Berkeley, 1989.
17 Raymond Williams, *The Country and the City,* New York, 1973, pp. 9-12.
18 Glazer and Lilla, *Public Face,* p.ix; Roger Scruton, *The Aesthetics of Architecture,* London, 1979, pp. 13, 15.

bond between architecture and life. For every Ruskin who saw architecture as the embodiment of spirit, there was a Thomas Hooker, the Puritan theologian who compared society's structure to a building's frame and the mind to a house, or a Roberts Vaux, who described the penitentiary system as a "noble edifice", and went on to discuss its foundation, its proportions, and its columns.[19]

Europeans carried these architectural metaphors wherever they went, building in the cheerful faith that a rightly ordered landscape could do much to create a rightly ordered society. This belief induced the sixteenth century Conquistadores to demolish the Aztec capital of Tenochtitlan and reconstruct it along European lines.[20] It stimulated English and French attempts to civilise Native Americans by building European-style houses for them.[21] It inspired the English choice of seats of government in India, the careful physical planning of imperial ceremonies, and the closely delineated Anglo-Indian architectural symbolism of the new imperial capital at New Delhi, which the historian E. B. Havell thought had the power to "reconcil[e] racial and religious differences".[22] It drove Arthur Phillip, Lachlan Macquarie and their successors to undertake ambitious building projects in Australia.[23]

This is a troublesome assumption. If we did not accept it, there would be little point in studying the history of the human environment, for unless we are merely antiquarians we must be interested, as Ruskin wrote, in "the powers of mind concerned in [the landscape's] creation or adornment".[24] But what exactly is the connection between the landscape and human values?

The penitentiary is a good starting point for considering this issue. Its builders were optimistic about their achievement. Although the systematic destruction of personality and identity in this intensely secretive, total environment links the reform penitentiary of the early nineteenth century with the twentieth-century concentration camp, its supporters – serious, religious, self-consciously

19 Thomas Hooker, *The Application of Redemption by the Effectual Work of the Word* [1659], in *The Puritans: A Sourcebook of Their Writings*, ed. Perry Miller and Thomas H. Johnson, rev. ed.; New York, 1963, 1:304; Roberts Vaux, *Notices of the Original*, and *Successive Efforts, to Improve the Discipline of the Prison at Philadelphia, and to Reform the Criminal Code of Pennsylvania*: with a Few Observations on the Penitentiary System, Philadelphia, 1826, p. 51.
20 Dora P. Crouch, Daniel J. Garr, and Axel I. Mundingo, *Spanish City Planning in North America*, Cambridge, 1982, p. 37.
21 Dell Upton, *Early Vernacular Architecture in Southeastern Virginia*, Ph.D. diss., Brown University, 1980, pp. 14-19, 29; Peter Nabokov and Robert Easton, *Native American Architecture*, New York, 1989, p. 57.
22 Bernard S. Cohn, "Representing Authority in Victorian India", in *The Invention of Tradition*, ed. Eric Hobsbawm and Terence Ranger, Cambridge, 1983, pp. 174-75, 195-200; Robert Grant Irving, *Indian Summer: Lutyens, Baker and Imperial Delhi*, New Haven, Yale University Press, 1981, pp. 76, 102, 104.
23 J. M. Freeland, *Architecture in Australia*: A History, Ringwood, 1968, pp. 29-30; Hughes, *Fatal Shore*, pp. 296-300; James Semple Kerr, *Out of Sight, Out of Mind: Australia's Places of Confinement*, 1788-1988, Sydney, 1988, pp. 11-15.
24 John Ruskin, *The Stones of Venice*, New York, 1883, 1, p. 38.

benevolent people – saw it as a model of humane rationalism. Its architectural form was held up as a social wonder drug. The Boston Prison Discipline Society declared that "there is such a thing as architecture adapted to morals; that other things being equal, the prospect of improvement, in morals, depends, in some degree, upon the construction of buildings," and that the cellular plan was the ideal moral building. They recommended that it be used not only in the penitentiaries, reform schools, and almshouses where it was already common, but also in "all establishments, where large numbers of youth of both sexes are assembled and exposed to youthful lusts," such as boarding schools, colleges, and the residences of large families.[25]

A copious literature produced by reformed convicts (a profession nearly as lucrative as that of reformed drug-users today) supported the image of the penitentiary as a model of the ideal urban society, the finest civic achievement of its era. Many middle-class nineteenth-century people were proud to have them in their neighbourhoods. Eastern State appeared regularly in the collections of prints and lithographs that constituted quasi-official urban self-portraits.[26] Penitentiaries were such popular tourist attractions that tickets were printed and admission sometimes charged. Eastern State was the most widely visited of all.

Nevertheless, moral architecture's record was mixed. Absolute isolation and absolute silence were difficult to enforce. Recidivism was high. Proponents of rival penitentiary systems as well as independent observers such as Charles Dickens argued that isolation created more lunatics than model citizens.[27] Most seriously, the keepers' own actions testified to architecture's inability to change convicts' minds, for they turned quickly to more direct methods of control. Within four years of Eastern State's opening, the legislature convened a committee to investigate the torture-deaths of several inmates. Although no one disputed the facts, the fatalities were excused as the regrettable consequences of dealing with hard cases.[28]

Stern imagery failed to deter crime and carefully planned spaces could not reconstruct many souls. Yet the penitentiary's shortcomings would be of no interest to us had its proponents not placed so much emphasis on the role of

---

25 *Fourth Annual Report of the Board of Managers of the Prison Discipline Society, Boston, 1829*, Boston, 1829, p. 55.
26 McElwee, *Concise History*, p. 7.
27 Charles Dickens, *American Notes* [1842], in *American Notes and Pictures from Italy, The Oxford Illustrated Dickens*, Oxford, 1957, pp. 99-100, 106-11.
28 McElwee, *Concise History*, contains the committee's report.

architecture: Haviland wrote that "the success of the System more than half depends on the construction of the prison in which it is attempted to be introduced".[29]   To what can we attribute its failure?

The difficulty lies in the problematical connection between architecture and its interpretation. Arguments for most civic architecture, whether it be ameliorative like a penitentiary or celebratory like a monument or a capitol, are commonly based on inadequate understanding of the relationship between artifacts and meanings. Meaning is socially negotiated and evolves with use; it cannot be established by proclamation. Yet this is what the builders of Eastern State did. They said this is what the prison means, and when we place inmates in it, they will respond like this. Some elements of the building will make them calm, some contemplative, some obedient, some industrious. They assumed a passive audience and they did not count on inmates who, as long as it stood, resisted the prison's argument, passively or actively, shirking or spoiling their work, devising means of secret communication, concocting and sometimes carrying off escapes.[30] They could not account for those driven mad by the environment or even for those who, far from seeing the penitentiary as a place of terror, found it preferable to the uncertainties of life outside, and committed minor crimes in the hope of being sent back.

We need not resort to claims of resistance to oppression (although that was part of the story) to understand the failure of penitentiary or of any other building to convey its message. Instead, we need to understand that the interpretation of the environment is ultimately more important than its creation. Literary scholars teach us that texts, as they like to call them, are abstractions until they are made concrete by their readers. No narrative can be complete, and the reader must supply the connections to "naturalise" what is inevitably a fragmentary account. When the glue of narrative convention is lost, the account fails to make sense, as everyone understands who has tried to read a medieval chronicle or a tale from a different culture.[31]

More important, the actions described have no significance until the reader supplies them. Since no society is homogeneous, since people are all different, we cannot specify the experience that readers will bring to interpretation.[32] Intelligence, psychology, physiology, and individual biography are all brought to bear on the text by the reader, giving it meaning. Furthermore, literary critics

---

29 Haviland to Tellkampf, 6:94.
30 Michael Capuzzo, "The Great Philly Escape", *Philadelphia Inquirer,* Apr. 28, 1988, p. 1-f.
31 Hayden White, *Tropics of Discourse: Essays in Cultural Criticism,* Baltimore, 1978, pp. 81-100.
32 Terry Eagleton, *Literary Theory: An Introduction,* Minneapolis, 1983, pp. 76-78, 120-21, 138.

like to speak of "intertextuality", meaning that we don't write or read ignorant of the contents of other works we have written or read. All this seems to me to be true of architecture, as well. We do not experience a building as an individual monument. We know it in comparison with the other buildings that surround it, in comparison with our bodies and our experiences, with other buildings we have been in, with other places and other times we have been in the same building. The reading of architecture is rendered even more complex because, unlike a text that we read with our eyes, we encounter the material world through several senses.[33] The geometrical perfection of a neoclassical space might be marred by the dissonant echoes that its dome generates or by the smells of a ritual performed inside it, its self-contained tranquility violated by intrusive street smells or noises, or by the contrast between the space and its occupants or uses. These are inescapable aspects of the experience of architecture. None can be controlled by the planner yet all affect the consumer's interpretation of the architext. No one can predict how architecture will be understood. Indeed, conflicting sensory experience may create an interpretation that renders the individual building meaningless as a unit of analysis.

Understanding interpretation in this way makes clear the enormous theoretical difficulty of promoting common architectural values. Nevertheless, it may seem terribly abstract and unconnected in any obvious way with the daily experience of the landscape. Common sense suggests that things are not quite as atomised as these comments suggest. There clearly are patterns in the ways buildings are perceived and used, just as there is sufficient agreement on language to allow us to speak, if not always to hear.

It is tempting to use these patterns to argue that they reveal common values that can serve as a base for reconstructing the civic. Certainly the Eastern State Penitentiary's builders lacked no confidence in their ability to define and build for the public good. They assumed that certain "divine and human laws" were, or should be, consensually accepted throughout society. Those who did not were deviants who would "not control their wicked passions and propensities".[34] Ruskin took the same stance in arguing that only those suffering from "some morbid condition of their minds" could disagree with his judgment.[35]

However, the architectural expression of common values has historically been limited in several ways, for example by ambivalence about the appropriateness

33 Dell Upton, "The City as Material Culture", in *Material Culture, World View, and Culture Change*, ed. Anne E. Yentsch and Mary C. Beaudry (Telford Press, in press).
34 Roberts Vaux, Letter on the Penitentiary System of Pennsylvania, *Addressed to William Roscoe, Esquire*, Philadelphia, 1827, p. 9.
35 Ruskin, *Stones*, 1:212.

of monumental construction. The struggle for public loyalty between beauty and economy is as old as republicanism. A late eighteenth-century traveler noted the Bostonians' preference for the useful over the "agreeable", which he thought inevitable in a commercial society.[36] In offering his design for the New Jersey state lunatic asylum, John Haviland denounced "useless and expensive ornament", arguing for a building "clothed . . . with that correct architectural Expression that the nature of Building & Oeconomy suggest is consistent with good taste and its Public Character".[37] In the same spirit, opponents of Robert Mills' Treasury building at Washington demanded that his "extravagant" edifice be replaced with "a substantial and economical treasury building".[38] This failure to see beyond the merely instrumental has been exacerbated, where buildings for the powerless are concerned, by the mean-spirited obsession with separating the deserving from the undeserving that Michael Katz has shown characterises the American approach to social welfare.[39]

Wariness of public building has not arisen from stinginess alone. Many Americans preferred modest building for ideological reasons. It was widely believed in the early nineteenth century that a republican landscape should exhibit a general sameness as a sign of common political purpose. "Luxury", or conspicuous differences in condition, would undermine the public spirit that a successful republic required. Early national Philadelphia's drab landscape was often attributed, not to "an indifference to the dignity and elevation of their city", but to a different kind of public spirit, expressed in charitable donations, scholarly pursuits, moral improvement, and attention to the streets and other mundane but necessary elements of urban life.[40]

The last point is an important one. Construction involves a choice among goals. So-called good architecture competes for resources not just with bad architecture, but with other non-architectural values. A recent visitor to Eastern State, for example, thought that "the city should let the Flyers and Sixers leave and use the money to fix it up". In other words, he preferred the survival of the building to the retention of the city's sports teams, recognising that both might not be possible.[41]

---

36 J. P. Brissot de Warville, *New Travels in the United States of America. Performed in 1788,* Dublin, 1792, pp. 109-12.

37 John Haviland, *"A Design for a Lunatic Asylum to Contain Two Hundred Patients with the Necessary Attendants Officers & Domestics",* Haviland papers, 6:104.

38 R. P. French, *Commissioner of Public Buildings, to R. McClelland,* Apr. 4, 1855, copy in Curator's office, United States Treasury Department, Washington, D.C.

39 Michael Katz, *In the Shadow of the Poorhouse: A Social History of Welfare in America,* New York, 1986, pp. 10, 18-19, 24-25.

40 *Philadelphia in 1824,* Philadelphia, 1824, p. 10; Brissot, *New Travels,* pp. 327-28.

41 Moran, *"Neighbors",* p. 6.

Here my points about fragmentation of interpretation and about shared patterns of experience intersect. What constitutes a common good? Interpretation is not atomistic, yet its most pervasive patterns trace cleavages of class, race, and gender rather than transcending them. These powerful contexts are the ones in which texts and buildings are most often read. Calls to commonality evade fundamental issues of power and its consequences in the landscape.

Thus our investigation of the public realm shifts from the question, "What values are to be celebrated?" to "Whose values are to be celebrated?" We return to the central issue of authority. In assessing the apparent absence of a mandate to build for the contemporary public, it is a mistake to see the great monuments of the past as evidence that such legitimacy once existed. The monuments of the past represent at best doggedness and as often outright arrogance in exercising power in the face of strenuous opposition.

Consider, for example, Philadelphia's city hall, an enormous building in the French Second Empire style. Covered by Alexander Calder with sculpture representing the natural and human riches of Pennsylvania and depicting the races of the world working together in harmony, the city hall is capped by a colossal statue of William Penn that by a so-called "gentlemen's agreement", violated only three years ago, stood taller than any other building in the city.

The city's government moved from quarters over the market house to Independence Hall shortly after the Revolution. By the 1820s, it was evident that new facilities were needed, and proposals and design competitions were mounted continuously for over forty years before agreement on a design and a site could be reached. Between 1860 and 1870, the architect John McArthur, Jr., weathered two separate, bitterly disputed public competitions and a third, private search to obtain the commission for the present hall.[42]

Conflict over the 1869 competition led the state to appoint a commission to choose the architect and oversee construction, to the dismay of the press, which assailed the self-perpetuating body as an undemocratic imposition. The enormous building rising on Penn Square was labelled "the marble elephant", "the tower of folly", "the great vampire", and "the temple of the taxpayer". In 1893, the mayor and some of his supporters seized the unfinished building and occupied it for several months in a futile effort to wrest control of the project from the state commissioners. The latter held on until the building was ready

---

42 The details in what follows are derived from John Maass, "Philadelphia City Hall, Monster or Masterpiece?", *AIA Journal*, 43 No.2, (Feb. 1965): 23-30.

for occupancy in 1901, seventy-two years after it was first proposed, and thirty years and twenty-four and one-third million dollars after construction began.

Even in the great age of civic building, public authority to build was more a product of arrogance and misuse of political power than of consent or cultural confidence. We must go on to ask why even arrogance no longer seems adequate to carry off such a project. Why has public building become more difficult? The answer, I think, likes in the democratisation of the body politic, as many writers have acknowledged.[43] Complementing the traditional republican aversion to display and the traditional capitalist stinginess has been a growing public suspicion of appeals to common values occasioned by the ways such values have historically been interpreted.

The difficulty lies in confusing conceptions of the public. Traditionally, several notions have coexisted. First, the public has been imagined as an entity separate from the citizenry, with its own rights and privileges, as in the ubiquitous signs that read "Property of the U.S. Government – no trespassing". Second, it has been seen as the common property of all the citizens, who are free to appropriate its benefits severally, as in the grazing or cutting of timber on common lands in the agricultural village. Third, the public realm might be held by the citizenry to be used in common, as in the parks and museums that most governments have established. Finally, the public realm might be seen as something lying between the last two, as a transparent medium of private endeavor. But all these meanings are abstractions except as they are realised in the landscape through social action. In social action we may "read" meaning. Citizens know that actions involve choices, and can see that historically the choices have reinforced systematically unequal rights and usages. They have good reason to be suspicious of appeals to commonality.

Let me show you what I mean. The fourth conception of the public, as neutral ground, was popular among prosperous nineteenth-century merchants and politicians. The streets should be free to all to use in ways that favored none more than others. On the face of it, this was an even-handed philosophy. Yet it obviously favoured those who had access to private space, as well as those whose business benefited from the ability to move about the city easily, at the expense of those whose businesses were too marginal to have a fixed location or too limited to require mobility. These included a variety of pushcart vendors and tradesmen and -women who sold low-priced second-rate goods. They were prosecuted sporadically, yet lithographs and photographs show that larger

43 See, for example, Glazer and Lilla, *Public Face*, p. xii.

businesses routinely spilled unchallenged out their doors, appropriating the streets and sidewalks as commercial space. In addition, while independent street sellers were accused of impeding traffic, merchants who rented space in Philadelphia's markets were allowed until the mid-nineteenth century to chain the streets on market days along a corridor that at its peak stretched, on two weekdays, a mile and a half east-west through the heart of the two-mile-wide city, and on two other days, a mile and a quarter north-south beyond the city limits. Similarly, for forty years the city's churches had the privilege of extending chains across the streets during services to prevent being disturbed.[44]

My point is not to suggest that long-nursed memories of old injuries lie behind public suspicion of appeals to common values, but to note the venerable roots of still-active assumptions about rights to public space. In recent years New York and Philadelphia have been the scenes of heated battles over the rights of vendors to sell everything from food to radios in the streets.[45] Irate letter writers describe pushcarts as "barnacles" that "block free passage on narrow sidewalks and . . . block visual access to the buildings they stand in the front of".[46] Yet few object to the equally obtrusive bollards and planters that the owners of up-scale office buildings erect to prevent the vendors' parking their carts on the sidewalks.[47] These are perceived as civic amenities.

What is presented as an argument for aesthetics and public access really represents differences of power and necessity in the definition of a public landscape.[48] While small entrepreneurs need to operate conspicuously and by direct appeals to customers, resulting in a "chaotic" commercial landscape, the élite entrepreneur operates by nuance, preferring an apparently neutral townscape in which overt signs of commerce are underplayed or absent. Bollards and planters are as much commercial blandishments as flashing signs and polished metal pushcarts. Through their regularity, subtlety, and above all by cutting down the density of use of the public sidewalks, they convey an image of gentility and restraint commensurate with the products office developers and up-scale shopkeepers sell.

The vendor wars are a manifestation of broader inequalities in the conception

---

44 "Legislature of Pennsylvania: Chains Before Churches", *Register of Pennsylvania,* 7 No.7 (Feb. 12, 1831): 111-12.
45 Hank Klibanoff, "Caught in the Crossfire of the City's Vendor Wars", *Philadelphia Inquirer,* Mar. 28, 1988, p. 1-B, 7-B.
46 Edward Harrison Bernstein, letter to the editor, *Philadelphia Inquirer,* Mar. 31, 1988, p. 20A; also letter from John M. Glennon, *Philadelphia Inquirer,* Nov. 15, 1987, p. 6E.
47 Hank Klibanoff, "Concord at 15th and Chestnut", *Philadelphia Inquirer,* Apr. 12, 1988, p. 1-B.
48 See Barbara Rubin's study of élite and small-scale urban commercial landscapes in "**Aesthetic Ideology and Urban Design**", in *Common Places: Readings in American Vernacular Architecture,* ed. Dell Upton and John Michael Vlach (Athens, 1986), pp. 482-508.

of public space. In a perceptive analysis of the high-rise development of Philadelphia, which threatens to engulf the major shopping district of Chestnut Street, the architectural critic Thomas Hine noted that "Chestnut Street is perceived as a problem, because it includes businesses that appeal to the vast majority of Philadelphians who do not have enormous amounts to spend . . . Chestnut Street is the main street of a poor and often polarised city. . . . There are many who would like to knock down Chestnut Street . . . , perhaps in the hope that everything lower-class will be pushed back into the neighbourhoods".[49] In short, not merely the use of public space, but the right to be there has been unequally interpreted.

Throughout the history of American cities, social diversity has seemed to be the most offensive aspect of public space. Women were thought in some quarters to be morally endangered by appearance in public where they could be addressed by members of other social classes and, conversely, as legitimate prey for harassment when they did use the streets.[50] Black people were often described as a threat to respectable passersby, although blacks themselves have been in more danger of violence from whites.[51] Most of all, working-class people were an offence to genteel sensibilities. "It is not pleasant", wrote one petitioner to the Philadelphia city council, "for every foot-passenger, whether Gentleman or Lady, promenading . . . either for exercise, or on a visit to a Building where the fine arts are being exhibited, to be perpetually Saluted by a Cab driver with the question 'Do You want a Cab?'" Such an experience would "deter ladies and respectable strangers" from going out of doors.[52]

Working people were made unwelcome in early nineteenth century parks like New York's Battery Park or Philadelphia's Washington Square by prohibiting such practices as smoking and reclining. New York's Central Park and the other great landscape parks of the late nineteenth century were off-limits to the active sports and games that working people enjoyed, to preserve the park for the passive contemplation appropriate to middle-class concepts of nature.[53] In cities like Worcester, Massachusetts, separate recreational areas for genteel and

49 Thomas Hine, *"Changing the Face of Chestnut Street"*, Philadelphia Inquirer, Jan. 24, 1988, pp. 1-I, 6-I.
50 Sidney George Fisher, *A Philadelphia Perspective: The Diary of Sidney George Fisher Covering the Years 1834-1871*, ed. Nicholas B. Wainwright, Philadelphia, 1967, p. 19; John Davis, *Travels of Four Years and a Half in the United States of America During 1798, 1799, 1800, 1801, and 1802*, ed. A. J. Morrison, New York, 1909, p. 355; Francis J. Grund, *Aristocracy in America from the Sketch-Book of a German Nobleman*, London, 1839, pp. 29-30.
51 Grund, *Aristocracy*, p. 29.
52 Edward Shippen Burd, Draft petition to City Commissioners on places assigned for cab stands, Feb. 7, 1842, Edward Shippen Burd papers, Historical Society of Pennsylvania.
53 Roy Rosenzweig, *Eight Hours for What We Will: Workers and Leisure in an Industrial City, 1870-1920*, Cambridge, 1983, pp. 136-40.

working people were institutionalised by the early twentieth century.[54]

Today, the homeless on the streets and in the parks of American cities are commonly depicted as obstructing, by their very presence, the use of public space by other people. Suburbanites fill the San Francisco newspapers with declarations that they will not come downtown while the homeless are visible. Early this month, the mayor of San Francisco had the police clear a homeless encampment from City Hall Plaza. The *San Francisco Chronicle* observed that "San Francisco's Civic Center Plaza suddenly looked like a public park –instead of a disheveled campground". Though there is room for complaint about some of the ways the park was being used, no such fine points interested the *Chronicle*, which noted that the action "cleanses one of the most visible signs of urban blight from the steps of San Francisco's City Hall". Its reporter found an obliging homeless man to declare that "this (the cleared park) is what parks are for. . . It was no good for children".[55]

I do not wish to debate the relative merits of particular governmental actions, but to identify a pattern. The values advanced as those of the public as a whole are invariably those of the genteel. There is no milder way to put it. The experience of urban public space has taught many citizens to read public architecture as a celebration of values that do not include them.

What does all this mean for the prospects for a revitalised public realm? We have seen that several theoretical and historical considerations render a simple correspondence between architecture and public values improbable. Architecture, like the "public", exists in the working out of social process; it is a political product, not an abstract medium that can elicit universal assent. Individual differences in response to architectural "texts" makes the relationship of architecture and values problematic, the varied historical experiences of social subgroups undermine the idea of a consensual public realm.

Is there no hope for a public realm, then? Do I end in cynicism and despair? That would be cheating. I think that we can grope our way toward an idea of a public, but I conceive it differently from most of my colleagues.

For one thing, like John Ruskin I would emphasise the notion of social process over visual design. Although he was notoriously obsessed with the minor visual details of architecture, Ruskin conceived architecture as a social art, celebrating

---

54 Rosenzweig, *Eight Hours*, pp. 128-36.
55 Marc Sandalow, "Homeless Ousted at Civic Center; Plaza Transformed from Campground to Park," *San Francisco Chronicle*, July 7, 1990, pp. A-1, A-16.

works that exhibited the soul of the workman and, as we all know, denouncing "the degradation of the operative into a machine".[56]

Yet the apparent populism of such statements is misleading. In a culture and in an author imbued with a deep belief in the connection between the material world and human life, we must be alert to Ruskin's language, which is permeated with metaphors of servitude. Ornament is a servant, sculpture a master. Ornament is confined in "happy submission . . . in accordance with its own nature".[57] It is no surprise that Ruskin's ideal worker also yields "obedience to higher powers", finding his "noblest state" in submission to another.[58] Ruskin is certain that noble servitude will flush illusions of freedom from craft workers' minds.[59] His idea of artistic value is profoundly hierarchical, even authoritarian.

Ruskin's comments remind us that any appeal to a consensual art is an appeal for cultural hierarchy.[60] The modernist reformers were rightly criticised for their top-down approach to what were otherwise laudably humane social goals. Most current critics of the public realm make the same mistake, offering mendacious appeals to popular taste while claiming to know what is best. In this they are no different from the modernists, except that their values are more suspect. They are certain that education of the public's taste will grant them the cultural authority they covet.[61] They presume that differences of landscape preference result from inadequate understanding, when they arise from a very precise understanding of the fissures that permeate our society.

It follows from this that I endorse a kind of cultural anarchy. Critics of the civic landscape often lament its chaotic quality, harking back to the mythical golden day when a commonly accepted architectural language unified the landscape and the people.[62] Classicism and the vernacular are held forth as evidence of societies at peace with themselves, but they are no more likely paths to building in the public realm than the great Satan modernism is.[63] Calls for a commonly accepted stylistic language simply miss the point about the meaning and experience of architecture. We cannot explain the alienation of an amorphous public from modernism by appeals to the inherent unlovability or incomprehensibility of particular visual forms.

56 Ruskin, *Stones*, 3, pp. 170-71, 2, p. 163.
57 See for example Ruskin, *Stones*, 1, pp. 238, 255.
58 Ruskin, *Stones*, 2, pp. 158, 164.
59 Ruskin, *Stones*, 2, 163-64.
60 Krier, *"Choosing"*, pp. 16-17.
61 Glazer and Lilla, *Public Face*, pp. xv-xvi.
62 Ruskin, *Stones*, 1:37; Glazer and Lilla, *Public Face*, p.xi.
63 Powers, ed., *Real Architecture*, pp. 16-17, 34; Helen Searing, *Speaking a New Classicism: American Architecture Now*, Northampton, Mass., 1981, pp. 9, 23-24.

Any style will do yet none can be adequate, because a reinvigorated public realm has nothing to do with style. The proper focus is on the landscape rather than the individual monument. It is for this reason that I have used the phrase public realm, meaning to encompass public architecture without being limited to it. Public action in space is more critical for understanding the public realm than the construction of imagery. The public face of architecture is a reflexive one, taking its meaning from the actions that occur around it and in turn annotating subsequent actions that take place in its presence.

Over time, meaning, some of it positive, some negative, attaches to the landscape. Thus, while I do not advocate tearing down the monuments of the past, which have accumulated their own heterogeneous meanings, neither do I think that we ought to build new monuments. If we look at the kinds of public action that seem to enjoy great favour these days – the ethnic and community festivals, the participatory sporting events, the farmers' markets, and other loosely structured gatherings – it strikes me that we need not great public buildings but great-meaning flexible, non-authoritarian - public spaces.

The problem with modern architecture, as we have heard, is one of scale, but the critical question is, scale of what? My answer is, scale of power, power to transform and to order the environment. The increasing concentration of power to change our cities in the hands of unaccountable entities, the imposition of too much order on too large a scale, is the proper focus of our criticism. Without romanticizing the society that created it, we might learn from public spaces such as the bazaar at Damascus. Its orderly, monumental, colonnaded Roman street was nibbled away during the middle ages and restructured by small commercial, social, and religious institutions of the new Muslim society. The result was a new order, arising from innumerable minor actions of the users replacing the top – down monumental Roman order. The old order was best understood in elevation, the new in plan. We might learn as much here in Melbourne by comparing the Regent Hotel's Great Space to Swanston Street. Vital cities are healthy cities. Rather than pine for a unified landscape of whatever style, we should promote its opposite. In a pluralistic society, a messy landscape is the healthiest. In a stratified society, a messy landscape is the most just.

PUBLIC ARCHITECTURE: THE OBJECT AND SUBJECT OF THE CITY, OR, GOOD BYE SINGULARITY AND TOTALITY!, HELLO MULTIPLICITY AND RELATIVITY!

Daryl Jackson

Part 1: Evolutionary Modern

In a prefatory note to his novel *Balthazar* of 1958, Lawrence Durrell comments:

> Modern literature offers us no unities, so I have turned to science and am trying to complete a four decker novel whose form is based on the relativity proposition. The first three parts interlap, interweave in a purely spatial relation.

> [And within the novel] We live [writes Pursewarden], lives based upon selected fictions. Our view of reality is conditioned by our position in space and time – not by our personalities as we like to think. Thus every interpretation of reality is based upon a unique position. Two paces east or west and the whole picture is changed.[1]

As you can see, to overcome the dreadful stigma of being a practising modern architect in this company of sociologists, historians and urban theorists I have had to produce a more elaborate sub-title and a quotation from a modern novelist to clarify my stance. The choice of the words "Hello" and "Good Bye" is intentional, for my disposition espouses an architecture of humanitarian values, rather than the purely technocratic pursuits which so many people now associate with modern architecture. My primary title indicates that the moral bias of this conference towards the "public face" of architecture can only be ignored at great peril to mankind, irrespective of the formal arguments we might attach to its manufacture.

From an historical point of view there are two Utopian architectural constructs. One is fixed, static and complete; the other is dynamic, incomplete and in a state of perpetual motion. Both are offered as "explanations" or "beliefs" about the nature of existence, with the state of scientific knowledge pertaining at the time seen as one limitation to the imagination involved. Architects have always been concerned with ideas about completion and totality, simply to ensure legibility and memorability of the object in space, as opposition to nature. But there have also been theories of "connectedness"; the consciousness of how

---

1 Lawrence Durrell, *Balthazar a novel*, E.P. Dutton & Company, Inc., New York, 1958, pp. i, 14. Copyright © Lawrence Durrell 1958

constructed objects assume new meaning as they become subject to the open space continuum through which we both move and stop. A city, composed of buildings and open spaces is one continuum, even though it is composed of a series of separate parts. Being able to remain fixed whilst knowingly being in a state of perpetual motion is one paradox that separates a modern world from that of the past. It gives rise to a relativity model which distinguishes the present.

By definition the act of architecture is transformational. Its material forms, public or private, are best informed by both subjective emotion and objective fact in the pursuit of the art. But don't be mistaken, architecture is not art: it is architecture. It possesses its own set of rules which range from the pragmatic resolution of shelter at one level to visionary symbolic expression, at another. Operating between these poles, Modern society evidences energies and emotions which continually ebb and flow in a state of uncertain symbiotic flux. We are only now discovering at the level of city management and planning just how complex our system of intellectual and practical demands have become. Appalling errors have been made within all the layers of thinking which comprise the modern city-state, founded as they are in Australia upon moral principles which at best seek to express a broad humanitarian and egalitarian value structure for the polis. Excellence is understood to be necessary, but only within a framework of social justice and democratic idealism.

It could be said that the true aim of social change for any society is the removal of conditions which inhibit the development and growth of cultural understanding. Modernism was born out of just such a value; the moral rejection of historic imitation, that area of thinking which Nietzsche called the "great wardrobe of time", and the compulsion to give a new (valid) expression to a new age. Adolf Loos believed that a Zeitstil (style of the era) cannot be created, it exists! (I take it this also means that it cannot be re-created). "All you have to do is learn how to discover it!" he said.

In a democratic state, the causal failings, whether they be in environmental degradation, atmospheric pollution, or in the building of the suburbs or the city may best be found in the subjective and representative workings of the culture itself, than in the objects so created and signified. And in a democracy everyone gets a chance to manufacture the *Zeitstil,* usually by attacking its existence to provoke change.

Broadly stated, the public face of architecture has been bruised and battered by two apparently disconnected factors, each based on a lack of commitment to evolving socio-physical ideology and vision about the purpose of the city. One of these factors is architectural and blame may properly be placed upon that threshold of modernism which barred any sense of historic continuity to demand an intellectual carriage of the art requiring total change in every circumstance. It was falsely argued that new technology, rationally expressed, would alone address the social ills of society lost in historic bourgeois borrowing on the one hand, and resolve the poverty of an industrialised working class living in overcrowded, insanitary inner cities, on the other. The second factor resides in the rising power of social free-will unleashed by even newer technologies attached to personal expression: individual affluence leading to a high level of mobility and choice of mass communications. Both of these have combined to fuel the flight to the suburbs; the worth of the city is no longer a key priority in the minds of those living in the outer ring, yet they are wired up to the whole world. Furthermore, there was the radical shift of emphasis in the 1960s towards "breaking down" the formal establishments and "de-institutionalising" the social process; those formal bodies which created the power symbols of the past (the generous public expression of the corporation, the city, the College, the University and the Church) went missing. It is also arguable that this society wanted greater equities expressed in the socially biassed new service programmes: health, welfare, education, public housing; all of which are in competition for a level of public funding apparently beyond our ability to provide.

The point of this discussion is to assert that, as a result of both these social and technical effects coming together at the one time, there has been no common desire to see the city (and its public architecture) assume the necessary significance (and investment) to get it right. The real concentration has been on a privatisation of the family, made self sufficient by affluence, two cars, a quarter acre block, a family room and two televisions. With all of this who needs a traditional city based as they are upon a socio-physical framework of pedestrian mobility, reinforced (in the nineteenth century) by public transport. Within the new *Zeitstil,* it is another kind of city.

Abdications of this kind have left the city in the hands of the commercial developer with architecture just a minor part of a "commodities stock" built for sale.

Further evidence of these circumstances may also be detected in the current form of city/government development packages or bids. Is the bid for the best price or the best architecture? Without articulated qualitative goals (or prior public consultation) such a process becomes purely "commercial" and "competitive". Success on the basis of "public accountability" is usually equated to "highest offer", irrespective of the architectural qualities. In such "development led" competition it is a matter of luck (i.e. pertaining to price) whether the best architectural result gets to be accepted. Unless the whole value system of the democracy demands it, the building form of the city will remain victimised by the limited perspective of economic philistinism.

In Australia, as in suburban America, most people live in what has been described by Joel Garreau, a senior writer for the *Washington Post*, as "Edge Cities". Nominated for a 1988 Pulitzer Prize for his reporting on emerging cities, and author of the best seller *The Nine Nations of North America*[2], Garreau urged American architects at their 1990 Houston conference to become the "guardians of America's edge cities". But with what fire-power, I ask?

The phenomenon of edge cities has developed, according to Garreau, because every American city that is growing, does so with multiple urban cores. Although this phenomenon began circa 1915 (aided by Henry's Ford), eighty percent of edge cities have been built in the last twenty years. A dominant characteristic of edge cities is that they are automobile-friendly, with more car parking places than public spaces, and few detectable "civic" symbols. The one gathering place, he asserted, is "the mall", because "it is privately policed, clean and safe!" Garreau maintains that edge cities truly are cities unto themselves, because they have urban complexity, diversity and size. An "edge city" he suggests will possess at least five million square feet of office space (which makes it larger than Memphis); six hundred thousand square feet of retail area (at least two large anchor shops and eighty shops); more jobs than bedrooms; is considered a separate "place" by local people; and was a "cow pasture" thirty years ago. "If it quacks like a city, it is a city", Garreau stated. "These areas are becoming their own urbs – they are not suburbs".

When Garreau was asked, "Will edge cities ever be civilised?" "That", he said, "brings us to the architect's role. I thought that architects built these places ... I later discovered that most edge cities are put together by the deal (zoning restrictions on building size and a developer's budget)." History indicates that innovative architectural forms are usually created by three factors which lie outside the mere consideration of style in any epoch. Two are technical; availability of materials and means of production; the third is the cultural context, in which a morality based upon beliefs usually mediates the physical expression of objects through the formulation of social or economic values. This essential "condition" today, reflects a hybrid, relativistic state of affairs which might best be termed "modernist/revisionist", with economic imperatives a salient value

2 Boston, 1981

for a secular society. And architecture, in its current pursuits, has to address as critique an apparently competing and diverging spectrum of values, ideas and attitudes: from public to private, from peripheral to purposeful argument, for a host of increasingly articulate cultural minorities, each with a particular point of view.

This is a world that the original modernists could not have contemplated. The "unity" once sought as a universal is no longer cherished as idea. More positive values are seen to emerge from a healthy (though infinitely more complex) "disunity", in which it is the architect's societal role to profess individual artistic authority. New-found value is continually based in ongoing exploration; the belief remains that progressive invention is necessary for each project and for each act of authorship. In such a search for an architecture of "ideas", pragmatic concerns continually need to be challenged by the poetic and intellectual. One key difference between a past modernism and the present resides in that important split between symbol and function, with the "symbolic" system of images assuming a greater significance than a merely utilitarian discourse allows.

No-one should doubt that while the mediocre performance of modern architecture may be attacked, so too can solutions that turn their back on the contemporary world to reproduce seriously either a fake Canaletto on-the-Thames or its more flippant kitsch cousins, wherever they persist as "historicist" reflections.

I am surprised to read quite justifiably-sound critique of populist modern architecture's failures, accompanied by an incredibly limited explanation of the causes; while an even more blinkered set of past propositions are supplied as an all too transparent remedy.

In my view the European city of the past existed as an intellectual spirit or idea, with its system of essential social assemblage seen as immortal: only architecture; building and rebuilding over the centuries is mortal. History cannot be redeployed as a future. The real traditions of mankind are based upon the idea of renewal and regeneration and we tend to forget that styles or images we now value because they are "historic" and familiar were once reviled and rejected. Possibly due to a naïve belief in a material world we have corrupted the spiritual issues attached to imagination and belief. Already through an inability to experiment and explore and to not commit ourselves to a future we have failed to accommodate the human spirit: there is a lack of nerve and the re-use of the past is a fetishism of the present.

Modernism has failed as a code firstly in its ability to convey feeling, and secondly in its inability to establish identity. This is particularly so in the centre city areas, which no longer are seen to possess valuable meaning or association. Houston gets to look like Boston and they both aspire to mimic Manhattan. There is a loss of identity. This we came to recognise as the so-called "death of Modernism". It caused the principal shift of emphasis in expressionism undertaken by a younger group of architects, following the first or second generation modernists. The first of these shifts has to do with lack of human signification or expression, the second with the inability to prescribe place, for within all the various and sometimes conflicting themes which characterise the whole period, the two constants which prevail are the attention paid to aspects of anthropomorphic form and contextual fit or association. Modernism had exhausted itself by concentrating not on the whole or multivalent part of its original charter, but by the development and belief of only one factor: the dictatorship of a technologically and fiscally biased bureaucratic world, with a cost/time machine aesthetic in charge. This is the fabric of modern internationalism – it's a nowhere world, and the vision, the truth, the beauty of the anticipated joy of modernism, is now a nightmare – like being in the palace at Versailles towards the end.

A re-reading of the revolutionary texts of Modernism indicates that this result was not intended. Gideon, the "father of the movement", considered the modernist code to have a four point programme.

1. Functional expression via truth to use, materials and technique.
2. The humanisation of the city ... this goal being a reaction against the social conditions of the poor.
3. The manifestation of a new monumentality, i.e.: the creation of buildings which symbolise man's social, ceremonial and community life.
4. Later (in 1954) he added "a new regionalism" in order to sustain a feeling of place.

Thus it is wrong (or too easy) to judge the intent of the modern movement merely by looking at the results. Society has forgotten that Paul Klee included the following dictum in the Bauhaus format: "obscuration, emotion, and fantasy are as important as function". Surely this combination of objectives has been ignored and the architecture of our times has been bought up on the stock exchanges as "commodities". Survival then, must be the manufacture of more powerful medicine – a new symbolism in the creative frame of human intelligence. The following excerpt from Susanne Langer *Feeling and Form: A Theory of Art*[3] is a healthy reminder of what is required:

---

3 New York, 1953.

The import of an art symbol cannot be built up like the meaning of a discourse, but must be seen in toto first; that is, the understanding of a work of art begins with an intuition of the whole presented feeling. Contemplation then gradually reveals the complexities of the piece, and of its import ... in art the complex whole is seen or anticipated first.

As an architect my concerns are about space, structure and light; and the human associations which attach to the tectonic culture of architecture. My methods of assemblage are inclusive: a spectrum of ideas which continually apprehend evolving and new demands for form. This leads to a complex inter-locking series of expression in which the process of authorship is manipulated to promote a dialogue between public and private, new and existing, association and idea, meaning and memory, identity and image. This is to promote an architecture biassed by a "critical intelligence", which sees "modernism" as an attitude towards enquiry (and not as style), developed in each circumstance by the chosen combination of inter-related ideas including the permitted social, typological and historical connections.

As L. A. N. Whitehead, writing in *Science and the Modern World*[4] about the nature of scientific enquiry, states:

All the world over and at all times there have been practical men, absorbed in irreducible and stubborn facts: all the world over and at all times there have been men of philosophical temperament who have been absorbed in the weaving of general principles. It is this union of passionate interest in the detailed facts with equal devotion to abstract generalisation which forms the novelty in our present society.

Such a "schema" reflects a desire continually to engage in an evolutionary urban dialogue whereby the past is encountered by the present to proposition the future. The making of a key architectural idea for each project is central: and just as a novel without a plot makes for dull or senseless reading, so does lack of architectural idea make for poor architecture, and it is here that cities the world over have suffered. Once again an excerpt from Susanne Langer is helpful to my argument about each design requiring theory to underpin its presence.

The building up of a theory – involves more logical considerations than people usually realise when they discuss methodology. It is not enough to survey the field of study, break it up into what seems to be its simplest constituent elements, and describe it as a pattern of data. Such a pattern is orderly, like an alphabetical index wherein anything known can be located, but it furnishes no leads to things unknown. To construct a theory we must start with propositions that have implications.

---

4 Cambridge, 1932.

The implication for an architecture of relevance to the present is not the totality, (meaning the internationality) we once may have been trained to think it was; but rather a universality in which principles of continuity and principles of change are constantly occurring, to be reinterpreted within an evolutionary context.

I started this section with a literary giant telling us he has "turned to science" to create a novel based on relativity. This is to suggest that in education the old split between art and science should be discussed in terms of the counter-productive "schism" it has created. The closing of this gap is necessary if we are effectively to manage our society. A major critique exists, not about our technical prowess, but rather, by the limits increasing specialisation has placed upon on our capacity to understand and manage the whole system of values.

We know that the best educated mind is one which will work on a multiplicity of levels. In reading a novel or listening to music our conscious intelligence draws on our sub-conscious reserves to create or "reconstruct" the personal emotional content or fiction of the activity in question.

To gain useful appreciation, interpretation and meaning, we are continually called upon to deliver judgment. This requires critical knowledge and creative imagination.

Part 2: Melbourne's Soul

As a text to commence this section of a discussion about Melbourne's urbanism, I want to quote from Gabriel Garcia Marquez' modern novel *One Hundred Years of Solit*ude[5]. "Science has eliminated distance" remarked the gypsy: "In a short time man will be able to see what is happening in any place in the world, without leaving his own house" and, over the page ... "Things have a life of their own" the gypsy proclaimed. "It's simply a matter of waking up their souls!"

There are two points to be made. First, that we do need Melbourne (and the other Australian cities) to have a distinctive and valuable "soul" and life of their own, to which the Australian residents feel attached. Cultural survival depends upon each generation being continually committed to keeping such a "soul" awake and alive. Second, that due to our advanced state of knowledge and our dependency upon a global scientific world, (of which we are part) we cannot ignore the activities and development taking place in the rest of the world. After

---

5 First published by Editorial Sudamericana, Buenos Aires, 1967; here quoted from Gregory Rabassa's translation, Harper and Row, New York, 1970.

all, as the gypsy informs us, we can see it without even leaving the house. This condition of "internationalism" or "modernism" is not new to Australians. We have always had to contend with such a prospect, even as we established the beach head cities and thrust inland for either pastoral or mineral wealth.

In taking this look at our own backyard, I want to reinforce that we do not live in an exclusive geographic realm either in Melbourne (or Australia); but rather, in a modern world of communications with a universal language and an increasingly interdependent series of intellectual, economic, and material exchanges at all levels in which, to survive, we must participate. My choice of the word "soul" is a conscious one, meaning that cities do convey an emotional and spiritual, even moral presence through the combinations of events and places that are the construct and the carriage of their civilisation. In my view Melbourne's "soul" is of the utmost national cultural significance. It exists in its art and in its architecture; in research and racing, football and finance, politics and pleasures, literature and landscape, religion and ratbaggery. Part of Melbourne's special merit is that it does stage magnificent major events, and it does possess a rich cultural archive in its city grid, and constituent institutions.

Most development occurs via a partnership between the corporate (intricate) city infrastructure and an individual or private activity. We therefore need to consider a dual set of values: the manufacture of a public enterprise or planned system of useful and sustainable development within which private or individual effort is anticipated, encouraged and included. Undoubtedly it is the combinations that count, with the quality of the city accruing from both the public enterprise and the private investment.

The point of this exercise is to assist you to see this duality; to acknowledge that everyone's contribution is significant and that Melbourne, as a manufactured nineteenth century city situated on the edge of a large body of water in an unspectacular river valley setting, really needs both the urban design of its public space and a qualitative architectural presence to support its immortality.

Imagine, if you will, Melbourne's beginning. John Batman, adventuring north from Van Diemen's Land in 1835 looks for water and pasture and a base from which to trade as a pastoralist. By 1837 the exchange with the Yarra tribes is done and Governor Latrobe has Robert Hoddle draw up the plan. Eight blocks by four, two hundred metre square, with thirty metre wide streets parallel to the river. It was a speculative plan, (the best) for the even grid provides a maximum of frontage for sale with the greatest efficiency. People were encouraged to leave London (and elsewhere) to buy up the city sections for tenure, investment and exchange one. This commercial speculative expression of the purpose of our cities (as opposed to say a historic, medieval city) is a fundamental aspect of its culture and has to be understood as part of the process. Everything is for sale!

Over time the layout and the topography, together with the foundation of public institutions and services, confer a differentiation of value as the key elements of a nineteenth century colonial existence are brought into play and the plan becomes a city.

Originally the better land value was in the West end behind the Customs House. Here was built the first Cathedral (on top of the hill) and the market place. Collins Street (above the mud and dust of the Yarra pool) becomes the key frontage and pushes further east towards Spring Street and the higher ground above the mud and dust of Elizabeth and Swanston Streets.

The river crossing at Princes Bridge makes Swanston Street the most important North-South connector bringing the botanic gardens and the affluence of a residential St Kilda Road into the city proper. The railways in Flinders Street conferred further commercial value. Flinders Street became a key frontage for the department stores. St Paul's and the Town Hall, the old Melbourne Hospital, the Library/Museum complex generated further civic importance to the Swanston Street axis. Collins Street hill above the Town Hall at Russell Street sees the twin churches precede the later ascendancy of the medical profession, both of which provide the vision of a new Paris. All these elements constitute the Melbourne we now know and presumably value as the tangible soul of the city.

Part 3: Workpoints of Relativity

We now live in a world in which consistency is not always possible and issues may vary significantly in relevance and importance. T. S. Eliot declared himself a royalist in politics, a classicist in literature, and an Anglo-Catholic in religion. In order to make the city work we now realise that, at a theoretical level, the "disunity" or "chaos" stems from a wider set of specialist discourses forming the value judgments. It is my understanding that intellectual survival depends upon our ability to pose hard questions, to challenge current orthodoxies, to explore and develop critique. I also believe that our thinking must be propositional, capable of being argued, yet "stabilised" as usable idea or theory. This is to suggest that formulation of ideas is normal and necessary for culture. The process involves the divergent pursuit of conflicting ideals, followed by convergent critique involving argument, and evaluation, advancing towards the conditioned idea. Without such a dialectic, future prospect is entirely diminished.

In other words, any advancement relies upon our culture, our literature, our art and our politics being full of contradictions, reversals and polarisations that have to be "worked out". It is a "paradoxical concept" requiring continual address. The necessary discomfort of intellectual oppositions represents the phenomenology of our time: namely the relativistic world of modernism in which we all encounter a range of values – national and international, technological and humanist, material and spiritual, physical and psychological, continuing and changing, private and public, individual and communal, even, moral and immoral.

This leads to the idea of this section of the paper arguing the values of the city from a series of specialised or focussed, generally pre-conditioned viewpoints; all of which, in a democracy, have to be apprehended.

1. The City as Polis

Like other western cities of its age, Melbourne has been persistently transformed since its very foundation. By this I mean that its life has been a continuous process of commencement and demand; decline and decay, rehabilitation, and rebuilding. Most of the central business district sites have been built over on two, even three occasions, with corners holding an ascendancy, mostly because (as any agent will tell you) two frontages are involved. All too often it is left to the laws of chance whether what is built captures the imagination, nurtures and sustains the dreams and brings a sense of pleasure, even joy, as well as answering the pragmatic demands for shelter, safety and security.

How do architects and their clients mediate in this free enterprise system, between public presence and private place? Are the urban arts some cosmetic to be applied to an economic land-use pattern, with profit the only motivating force? Can Australians look forward with pride or pleasure to enriched urban experiences in their cities as well as to pursuing the social goals which are the qualitative hope of a post-industrial world? These questions reflect the failure of the separate forces involved to be harnessed by their interdependency; the provision and designation of public open space, changing transportation systems, services and utilities, retention of the old and valued streetscapes and buildings; the development of the new. Currently an enormous gap exists in the way the Australian urban landscape is being developed and experienced. There is no generally agreed theory about urbanism, artistic or not. And our way of city or town building remains rooted in the ideas that function begets form, that programmatic understanding secures expression, and that economic accountability is the key qualifying factor. This is tangibly illustrated by the fact that in Melbourne, one major Australian city which does express a vision of civilisation and culture, it is the historic nineteenth century parts of the city and gardens that we show to visitors as substantive distinguishing elements of our urban culture. The mediocre expansion of the past fifty years is not a consideration, lest it be also handsomely endowed with landscape. Therefore, in order to excel we need a much closer bonding of intention and appreciation at various levels of design – between an articulate public and its politicians; between planners, architects, and artists; between the public and the private realms.

At one level of endeavour the design of the city is about establishing local, popular and particular cultures; and at another, it is about creativity and originality; provocative and heroic investigation.

2. The City as Public Territory

As an urban city which needs its architecture Melbourne represents Australian civilisation even more positively than any imagery of beach or bush, flora or fauna. If we have not understood the struggle for our urban identity it is largely due to a misplaced perception of its worth and our own enterprise and skill in its manufacture. Melbourne in the 1860s to 1880s was an astonishing urban phenomenon. It is possible to argue that no other city of its population reached the intactness and richness, both cultural and intellectual as well as physical, with such energy, confidence and fervour.

Today, there is a similar challenge in the inner city to build responsibly and well, anew, caring for critical items of heritage, affording a better prospect for the future. Most Australians have no metaphor for "city" and get no peak experience from it, either as a place of personal activity or of substantive art. The inner city is relegated to a place to visit; the parks, museum, and sporting arena. As place it is not functionally appreciated or consciously "possessed" in the European sense. And, as our early cartoonists readily portrayed, there has always been suspicion of the "city slicker". Is it fair to hypothesise that Australians in cities are as uncomfortable as their forebears were in the natural and alien landscape? Australians no longer inhabit a univalent social or static framework such as might have existed pre-World War II. We now reflect diverse and fragmented sub-cultures, each with a distinctive or special view of a multivalent whole. This is an important fact for architects who wish to profess to their contemporaries, and an important positive development in an Australian society which has dramatically changed over the past thirty years.

There are now sufficient numbers of inner-city, suburban, and country groups for cultural metaphors to develop about each grouping. The former dominance of the Anglo-Scottish-Irish orthodoxies has diversified through the pattern of later immigration (much of it Asian) and there exists, albeit not in a large degree, a richer, more urbane cultural format. One could be most optimistic about it. Ironically, the only real unifiers remain our continuing dislike of authority or control mechanisms (e.g. politicians and police), and our absolute preoccupation with sports – particularly those we can win. In fact, *winning* is our national sport.

The relevance of city as public territory and form is as old as the hills upon which people first assembled, and our role is to build imaginatively; to make the city and the suburbs both livable and lovable. Paradise, you will recall is pictured as man and landscape observed together, and intrinsically linked via a figurative and operative narrative which characterises, explains, sustains and makes memorable the circumstances of life. The primary purpose of any city is its own monumentality.

3. The City as Habitat

If the psychological setting for Australians is bound up with landscape, the physical setting is not. The majority have always lived in the city, and, as soon as transport made it feasible, in the suburbs. As "reality", the suburb is the half-way world in which most Australians, given preference, choose to live. Insofar as appreciation of the landscape is concerned, most Australian suburban home gardens and public parks until the 1960s were planted out with imported European species. Australian plants have only recently (since the 1960s) become an accepted metaphor as a civilizing or mediating factor. The suburbs are an *almost* world, certainly not London or New York, but in the imagination, at least, an approximation. They are also an approximation of country or pastoral existence – a micro squattocracy on one's own quarter-acre settlement. Real or absolute city form is not desired; nowhere do we find in the history of Australian culture (other than among the few intellectuals to emerge, and who maybe went elsewhere to satisfy their need) a popular consciousness for a physical expression of polis. Even today most Australians reject the inner city as place of residence; not for them the hustle and buzz of the crowd, the idea-making of the street.

The real Australian, the dinkum middle-of-the-road, honest, straight and true hedonist, is a suburbanite. His physical world is the half-garden, half-house (neither splendid works of art, but demanding considerable time and effort), with holidays spent in even lesser built form – experiences: a tent or shack on the coast. But this is no mere retreat to the bush or landscape as natural reawakening. There is a power boat for water skiing (walking on water) and four-wheel drive or trail bike to conquer the bush, if not obliterate it. Some believe that in the layers of suburbia, laminated onto the historic core in a period of post-war expansion there exist no further ideas beyond the apparent freedom of life on the quarter-acre block and the free-standing villa. Others, however, believe enormous untapped energy is trapped in the suburbs awaiting some form of new-found release. If only this were so, for beyond the sports metaphor that is apparent, what is desperately demanded is a sense of place for all the other things that happen there.

As "edge city" material Melbourne's outer suburbs are characterised by a myopic placelessness, recognisable only as a grid of "intersections", with a sea of cars around the shopping "centre", or separately located civic centre, or separately placed school. Very few of these establishments possess a critical architectural presence, by way of town or collective polis. If you are not able to drive, you pay an enormous penalty. Even the good old strip streets like a Puckle Street, Moonee Ponds or a Burke Road, Camberwell are missing, and the whole assemblage of elements is afloat in a sea of "open space" such that important linkages between events of a communal nature are lost, except upon those who participate.

4. City as Heritage

The inhabitated sector of Australia is no longer "natural". Increasingly large sectors of Australia are cultivated by "man made" activity, the result of both purposeful and conscious ideas and activities, bound up with intentions and exigencies of past and present.

To know Australia is to know the history of Colonial establishment and social progress; of land tenure, pastoral and industrial activity; of urban form; and, above all, of the umbilical linkage to "home". What is really critical about, and special to, the Australian psyche, is the feeling of being on the *edge* (of Western culture) rather than in the *centre*. This sense of extended or apparent remoteness has done more to characterise our consciousness of "existence" than any feeling for or against aborigine or landscape.

My purpose here is to offer prospective discourse; a search, a questioning, a commentary about Australia's urban values in an attempt to draw together a model of those special bonds which generate our feelings for city and suburb, beach and bush, the *urbs* and *rus* of Antipodean western civilisation.

Two critical questions emerge: is there a compelling Australian urban tradition, and can the sub types which constitute the different parts of Australian cities be intensified? Does the future of Australian architecture reside in our perceiving the intensity of its culture: the need to be incisive about the synthesis of a technological world of knowledge, and the emotive condition of place? Arguably, there are five prototypical physical models: the wilderness, the country side, the institutional centre city, the historic inner suburbs, the outer suburbs. Each type projects a different physical morphology, yet each type possesses people within it of similar behavioural, social and political persuasion. Each demands a differing physical understanding and solution. Our prospect is to heighten the difference.

5. City as Art and Architecture

Any critique of the modern city must address the ideals and ideas of art: questions of principles and intentions, not just of materialism and pragmatism. Cities are not simple socio-functional mechanisms linking habitats of home, work and recreation via a transportation system. They have also to offer opportunities for life to develop and excel, to be seen as signifiers of culture, as treasure-houses of shared and valued human experience.

This is to suggest that the urban arts, inclusive of planning, architecture and design are not abstract, technological elements of city building that can be independently pursued without regard for the whole composition.

For cultural and historic reasons, Australians have largely ignored the emotional necessity of the city and have been suspicious of its prospect. At the most popular level they have preferred to concentrate their dreams and aspirations on the "open space" mythology of the bushman, the supposedly naïve, intrinsically capable, (actually streetsmart) Crocodile Dundee. In my view current Australian mainstream culture has avoided the "metropolitanism" of life in the city, preferring their "own" place in the suburban tracts which surround the historic core. In doing so a new form of city has been established : one that is not convergent or concentrically constructed (as it once was), but is now an even network of events, with a life of its own, interpreted and made real via the communications grid.

Part 4: Judgement: The City As Enterprise

Any value system is continually under attack, change is constant, and rapid change is structurally part of modern consumer society. In the 50s, the city was still symbolically the control centre of commerce and culture, fed mechanically by the spokes of the concentrically focussed transportation system. By the 60s, the city was losing its central grip and much of its bustling life, as suburban centres were built up as detached, faceless internationalism to contain city-like function in objects that looked like warehouses and were euphemistically known as supermarkets. The office block, dead at night, came to symbolise the city. In the 70s development intensified, and only the self-assured were prepared to persist with misguided ideas of urban living in the inner-city terrace or apartment. For the vast majority it was to be another layer of terracotta on the perimeter. In the 80s, we have no trouble in thinking of the city as a place to be, only now we must learn (yet again) to cope with both its confusion and its contradictions.

Australia has inherited its full share of modernist dogma, bureaucratised and misunderstood here as much as anywhere else in the world. The results are plainly seen in the newer post-war suburban developments which rigidly set apart shopping centres, schools, churches, civic buildings and parks into zones which are not allowed to contaminate residential and industrial areas.

In the light of this, perhaps its not incredible that the last thirty years of building in Australia have seen no major instance of urban formation. There have been attempts, of course: Mt Druitt and Campbelltown in NSW come to mind as brave tries. But you wouldn't go out of your way to visit them. So, it is no coincidence that the most perceptive present day architects and youth alike have turned to the city and its old inner suburbs for signs of urban life. The city is recreating itself, is being recycled as another era celebrates and values urban culture. Architects, those who are observant enough, will be able to analyse what makes the city work. Some will be surprised to realise that urban culture is generated not just by composing individual buildings and setting them adrift in the amorphous open space of the suburb.

Unfortunately, the format of the outer suburb is not designed by anyone in particular. Its anonymity is assured by the process that is used to develop it, and we are none the better for it. There are no edges, and no centres of significance, just an even spread of imposed surface of no substance, made memorable only by the signage.

Here, in summary, is a seven point programme.

1. In Melbourne there has always been a convergent, articulate, formidable urban tradition. Its content and its form closely parallels matching configurations of western intelligence wherever they have been applied. It remains valuable.

2. This tradition is, by definition, essentially Anglo-Saxon in its cultural base, yet modified by a distinctive attitude towards "open space" as representative of privacy, individuality and freedom.

3. Land ownership as commodity is a key factor, promoting a sense of identity and security.

4. The Australian ideal relates to concepts of equal opportunities for everyone, leisure as well as work, and the suburban city form most clearly reflects such values at the private level and avoids them in the public realm.

5. No-one is designing the public space and face of the city, and there is absolute need to review and rethink the manner in which the architecture of the larger metropolitan frames is being achieved. One former framework was to hang it on the public transport route. Without this prop a new powerful, formal imagery about the public and communal zones of the suburban city needs to develop, in order that we may learn to celebrate and value each other, not just the artifacts we possess. This means setting to work on the pattern of mobility and of provoking as figurative objects all the components of the city so that it has both meaning and memory.

6. The form of the city itself is crucial as object and not just as a subject of its architecture. This means that each building plays a role both in the sky and at the ground/street level. In the sky the building is a landmark; in the street it is a social opportunity, and place of formal engagement. There is a private obligation to the public realm and it is the conscious and moral endeavour of architectural intelligence to manifest it.

7. Notwithstanding any of the foregoing, the best part about living in Australia is that one always suspects that its future is going to be more important than its past, and that "incompletion" is one of its best values.

It's as well to remember that the prime purpose of a city is as a place for people to congregate, aggregate, and construct their social networks and cultural identity. The real point of city life is to celebrate human presence. It is the role of architecture to make this apparent at all levels of engagement. This paper commenced with Lawrence Durrell's *Balthazar* and it ends with this observation from *Justine*. "It is the city which should be judged though we, its children, must pay the price".

6 Lawrence Durrell, Justine, EP. Dutton & Co., Inc., New York, 1957, p.13. Copyright © Lawrence Durrell 1958

THE PUBLIC FACE OF ARCHITECTURE OR THE FACE OF PUBLIC ARCHITECTURE?

Hans Hallen

Jose Ortega y Gasset described our age in his *Revolt of the Masses* written in 1930, in this way:

> Towns are full of people, houses full of tenants, hotels full of guests, trains full of travellers, cafés full of customers, parks full of promenaders, consulting-rooms of famous doctors full of patients, theatres full of spectators, and beaches full of bathers. What previously was, in general, no problem, now begins to be an everyday one, namely to find room[1].

This society, the "masses" of Ortega's book, are our public. It is for them that the public squares, sports stadiums, "festival" markets, themed shopping centres, and exhibition halls are created.

What they see as they move around is the face of public architecture. This is an architecture that is intended to impress, titillate, and please the masses. It is the subject to which rulers apply their building energies and creative skills. But it isn't the only architecture and in democratic societies the emphasis changes from a concern for the face of public architecture to the idea of the public face of architecture. This is my focus in this *Conversazione*. In simple terms what we see as we drive in to Melbourne or Sydney from the airports is the public face of architecture. It is an ever changing visual scene, to some eyes chaotic, and by various canons of taste, ugly.

That ugliness in the past has been paralleled by critiques of the ugliness of social circumstances. Existing buildings and urban environments have been seen as ready for demolition because they have contributed to degrading conditions for living. I do not need to comment greatly on the history of planning reforms, of bye-law changes and the practical and symbolic ideals that contributed to the attitudes that have had such a great part to play in post World War II reconstruction and building. As it is true that the shape of cities and the character of their architecture mirrors the political ideas that dominate a period, I will draw from my own experience.

I worked as a young post-graduate for the London County Council on its model housing estate - the Roehampton Lane project. Built on the combined land of

---

1   Authorized translation from the Spanish, New York, W.W. Norton & Company, 1932, pp. 11-12.

two great Georgian houses with their "Capability Brown" gardens, they were well designed and impeccably detailed, and well constructed. They consisted of a dozen apartment towers of twelve floors each, five slab-like buildings standing in a row with splendid views over Richmond Park, set within beautiful gardens. In short, they were a model of modernity, which is building the best way you can, and of modernism, the idea that society is perfectable: that was the social model that directed the architects' and planners' brief.

I visited Roehampton again recently and found no visible disasters of social depravity nor of architectural collapse. The estate had become integrated into the general fabric of that part of the city and contributed to its richness and diversity. This was in contrast to what I saw in Manchester on the same visit to England. There I saw 5 fifteen-storied residential buildings in the process of being demolished. These buildings less than twenty years old, showed evidence that some occupants had set fire to their own apartments. The demolition was the last despairing gesture by the authorities to rid itself of a massive economic, social and political problem. These dramatic actions heralded the end of "social" housing as we know it. For a time the failure of these buildings and the social problems they presented were thought to derive from their design. While the design may have been imperfect it has become increasingly clear that it was the limited control the occupants had over their environment that triggered the reaction. Lack of choice and bureaucratic building management are two of the problems. Brought up on a diet of arguments based upon Calhoun's experiments in the 40s with rats (crowding them together developed antisocial behaviour), architects and planners believed that crowding was the problem and that publicly owned and designed buildings were part of the answer. But as we know, in a democratic age those for whom we build are not Emperors or Kings or bureaucrats but people much like ourselves.

After my disconcerting visit to Manchester I visited the street in Macclesfield, Black Road, where Prince Charles started his journey on his path to seek a new architecture. Black Road, with its broken down miners' houses was a physical and social sink. A leaderless, apparently helpless and in the main unemployed community was to be rehoused, relocated and saved by a planning authority. The planning authority, using the laws available, would demolish the existing housing and new housing would be provided elsewhere for the disadvantaged who lived there. It was not to be. Rod Hackney, then a post-graduate architectural student living in the area, helped to mobilise a willing community successfully to resist the demolition.

In the end the buildings were retained and those who lived there renovated their houses, achieving in the process both self esteem and a sense of purpose. I met the chairman of the committee that had undertaken the process of renewal and renovation. He was in his seventies, a retired carpenter, and had a history of long periods of unemployment. The challenge of leading a street committee in fighting for the preservation of their homes revealed qualities of leadership that otherwise would have been dormant. Ownership and user control of the housing environment has replaced distant bureaucratic control of housing everywhere, and with this has come a change in the architecture. It is smaller in scale and richer in choice. And we have also gained more knowledge and understanding of the effects of crowding on behaviour. As Freedman in his *Crowding and Behaviour*[2] has described it – crowding on its own is not harmful – it only tends to enhance a particular experience. Human motivation and the development of self esteem are much more important than physical conditions.

In South Africa, where I have lived most of my life, I have witnessed the conflict between architectural modernism and architectural liberalism, with their contrasting views of the role of the individual in society. The modern movement of the 1920s and 30s in Europe had a profound effect on South African architects. In the early 1930s a group of young architects responded to the excitement of its approach, to the sweeping away of older forms of building in parallel with what were seen as socially undesirable forms of living.

The apparent hopefulness of modernism, architecture as a tool to wipe away social pathologies of the worst sort, gave energy to a remarkable school of architecture. Some of these architects befriended Le Corbusier and he, in a modest and sensible letter written in 1939, encouraged them. A feeling for the time is illustrated in Anatole Kopp's work on the modern movement in Russia in the 1920s, *City and Revolution*. In it are spelled out the major forces- creative, socially-improving, scholarly and scientific, organisational and political – that inspired the era. Many creative people had rallied to the promises of socialism in the 20s and 30s, and much that was of enduring value was produced then.

It may be enough to say that the idea of keeping and restoring historic monuments, developing building standards in a scientific manner through national building institutes, and registering architects by a national state authority, had their most powerful support and initiation in the Russia of Lenin and Stalin. Modernism in architecture, driven by political ideals that emphasised central authority, shared with a liberal view of architecture the ideals of functional modernity. Modernity in this sense is simply the best way to build. South African architects of the '30s, '40s and '50s pioneered strongly centralised institutions such as the National Building Research Institute, and

2 San Francisco, 1975

explored planning and architectural initiatives that would accommodate a future urbanising and mainly black society. And it was in the 1940s and early 1950s that the major prototypes and planning ideals for South Africa's black townships were conceived. The townships, planning ideals conceived on a socialist and "top-down" planning approach were taken over by the Nationalist government when they came into power and it need be no surprise to learn how easily these plans fitted the apartheid policies of that government.

What was surprising at the time (1950s) was the abandonment by some of the brilliant young architects of the 1930s of the style of modernism. And much as modernism in architecture was replaced by neo-classicism in the 1930s in Russia on the orders of Stalin, so in the 1950s new, well-built, neo-classical buildings of a similar style were being produced in South Africa. For those who today call for the return of classical detail, cornices and all, let me say, we had quite a bit of it then – albeit in a humourless and desiccated manner. Town plans for parts of some cities, in particular, of Cape Town, were produced by planners sympathetic to this type of formalism. Old Victorian buildings that were no longer useful would be demolished and in general, a formalist planning approach dominated.

This was also true in the case of the Black Townships. The plans for these were prepared on the neighbourhood planning precepts of English town planning of the 1930s and special types of houses were designed. The houses were remarkable for their functional efficiency and for their cultural neutrality. None of those who have seen the houses of Soweto can ignore a feeling for what they look like. The townships were eventually to become the focus for social revolt. The houses were seen as symbols of poverty and degradation. As in Manchester, houses were not burnt because they were ugly, but because they represented the nearest available target on which to display deep-seated frustrations.

For those familiar with the 60s, and early 70s saga of urban renewal in England and America it will be of interest that the South African government studied the laws and workings of urban renewal in England and America as it sought to implement its Group Areas Act. The process is well known, and the wasteland area in Cape Town called District Six, adjacent to the Central Business District, is the most infamous example. All the "Coloured" persons who lived there were moved out in keeping with the Group Areas Act, using the well known stages of urban renewal i.e. the identification of a run down area, the freezing of development, with the effect of locking the community into a period of self-fulfilling degradation, followed by demolition. This approach is now properly in disrepute everywhere, and has been fundamentally rethought. District Six in

Cape Town and similar areas stand as testimonies to the failure of such planning policies. They are only made more dramatic by government policies that regard political rights and access to opportunity on a racial basis. Modernism, totalitarianism, top-down planning policies, and the attitudes that prop them up are really all the same. This experience of the architecture that results from the centralising and socialist planning policies is one that is shared by many – it certainly is not unique to South Africa.

In contrast with this approach to building there has been over the last thirty years or so what can best be described as a liberal view. The emphasis of its approach has been firstly to question many of the rules of centralised and doctrinaire planning, arguing for the need to leave well alone, to emphasise the individual and his needs and rights in planning and development. In practical terms in the City of Durban (where I have spent much of my working life), a small group of architects working as advocates for this point of view have been able to achieve some changes in City planning and development attitudes. These include the establishment of policies that develop the shopping arcades and lanes of the CBD into a rich web of shops, large and small, in what is largely a pedestrian area. The old railway station near the city hall has been converted into a shopping area with 180 shops, and a disused area has been converted to a new city park that is seen as safe, and as they say, "user friendly". Housing laws have been altered to encourage medium density and in the main low-rise housing, and Indian temples and historic monuments have been preserved and reused. More than this, architects have been involved in the creation of City arts and cultural programmes. These were the results of the efforts of unpaid private individuals seeking changes in the way in which the city was governed. As a consequence, the architecture itself is also changed. In the CBD access by the public, in particular the pedestrian, becomes of prime importance; the individual must be shaded from sun and rain, with easy and safe access for all to the marketplace.

The response by architects and those who brief them to these values is now in its early stages of development. But in my view all building types and environments will be changed thereby, as there will be developments in building technology, new materials, and systems of management. So the city will become not a succession of glass lift-lobbies but a succession of places open to the arcades and passages of the older city, and organised in a manner that requires new developments to recognise the existing fabric and to develop and enhance them.

Where are the ideas of this architecture to be drawn from? Not greatly from the vocabulary of the past, for in the end history rides at the architect's elbow, and not in a text book at his side or in a faxed injunction. Crafting the best materials, new and old into assemblies made with structural efficiency, he will produce buildings that respond to the myriad signs and symbols that a society produces and needs. And those symbols have scarcely been sought or acknowledged by architects. It is a telling truth about our times that MacDonalds and Disney have a more acutely attuned eye to what those signs are, as have the car manufacturers such as BMW.

Colonial and post-colonial societies adrift on the periphery of great metropolitan cultures suffer the problems of isolation. And here, if big business wants a building of prestige and importance, or, as has already been argued, a mayor of a progressive city wants something "good", where better to go than abroad? Styles and fashions waft on down from distant metropolitan cultures. It may be flippant to say that post-modernism is the modernism received in the post, but there is a truth there. I do not argue for the homespun but I do argue for the development of bold, practicable ideas based upon a deep knowledge of the possibilities of our cities.

Lutyens and Baker came to India and brought, not just their prowess as architects, but also a sense of staying for the longer term. Observing how things were done in India, they could draw upon those building traditions that were useful. In the process they helped develop sections of the construction industry. It was more than a short visit with designs sent in a roll. It was done so that the best of what there was could be fused to what they brought with them. Baker did the same in South Africa. He helped to alert his colleagues to the virtues of the 17th century Cape architecture, particularly in terms of its practicality. In building his large new buildings he saw to opening old quarries and created new and appropriate working details for his buildings and trained new skills in building and design.

This is a time when cities in Asia, Africa and in Central and South America are growing at a pace, and to a size beyond known precedents. Those are not the places to be guided by the steady development of Georgian England, by the sensible style and practicality of Jefferson, the authoritarian management technique of Haussman, Sixtus and even Stalin. Ours is an age more like the Elizabethan than the Georgian. There is both ugliness and creativity in these cities, and their growth and vitality will leave none of us unaffected. We can respond best by a forward looking approach that seeks to capture in built form the aspirations of society – a diverse and complex society with an equally complex cultural heritage. The idea of a single cultural tree stem feeding on Western ideals is gone for ever. If we need a new metaphor there is one from "Paradise Lost" that is more appropriate. Milton, looking for a tree that would provide shelter and clothing for Adam and Eve chose the Banyan Tree – or as it is known in Southern Africa, the Wonderboom (wonder tree). It did not have one stem but many!

> "Into the thickest Wood, there soon they chose
> The Fig-tree, not that kind for Fruit renowned,
> But such as at this day to Indians known
> In Malabar or Decan spreads her arms
> Braunching so broad and long, that in the ground
> The bended Twigs take root, and Daughters grow
> About the Mother Tree, a Pillard shade
> High overarcht, and echoing Walks between;
> There oft the Indian herdsman shunning heate
> Shelters in coole, and tends his pasturing Herds"[3]

The accent on appropriate shelter, structure and the choice of this particular tree with the intertwining of the practical and the symbolic is too pointed to ignore. The new architecture is not a mask. It is of the forest where when you provide shelter or make it we can say with Thoreau –

> "Better Paint your house your own complexion;
> let it turn pale or blush for you...".

---

3   *Paradise Lost,* IX, VS. 1100 - 1109; *The Poetical Works of John Milton,* ed. Helen Darbishire, Oxford University Press, London, 1960, p.210

PLANNING AND ARCHITECTURE AT THE END OF OUR CENTURY

Harry Seidler

Disenchantment must surely be the appropriate word to describe what most people in cities of the western world feel about the newly-built developments taking place around them. Not only are the physical problems obvious – the overbuilding with excessive bulk, the consequent pollution, traffic and pedestrian congestion – but the visual impact is undistinguished at best, oppressive at worst. Due to increasing urbanisation it is an environment that is being added to constantly and which will, almost certainly, worsen in time. Indexes of how much is allowed to be built are based on political decisions taken by elected city governments after lobbying by pressure groups of landholders and developers. The latter see their role as purely one of responding to the growing market demand for floor space. What flows from this are long-term profits and capital growth for investment in a time of inflationary devaluation of liquid assets.

Given immense thrust through the media, the emerging new laws and images make us believe that the direction of development in the last eighty years or so has been totally ill-oriented – that it has created nothing but environmental and visual chaos. It is put to us forcefully that the time has come for a complete turnabout; we should abandon all past notions of city planning, discard theories of architecture developed in our time and change direction totally. This anti-intellectual stance is nothing other than an irrational turning back of the clock away from the gradual, logical and consequential development of this century. To understand how deeply this reaction has permeated current attitudes towards the built environment, let us examine two areas of concern – firstly, what is allowed to be built in our cities and secondly, what architects choose to build.

1. The Urban Dilemma

In the realm of urban planning, it seems that all the proposed utopian schemes for guiding three-dimensional physical planning after World War II have not been pursued. The enlightenment needed to grasp the benefits, and consequent rewards to the community, was too much to expect. Landholders fought against constraints on building bulk for fear of depreciated property values without compensation. Politicians found the necessary actions of resumption and re-subdivision "untenable". So, *laissez-faire* attitudes prevailed and development has lurched forward on the assumption that market forces alone are best left to guide it.

The physical results of rejecting far-sighted policy has led, inevitably, to a negative public reaction. This, in turn, has been given widespread momentum by the media which purvey and encourage conservation modes. The outcome is that any proposal to build something new is immediately put on the defensive. The call is either for abandonment of entire projects or the preservation of existing buildings and their re-use. Where this policy is applied to worthy structures of the past it is obviously desirable and to be encouraged. But the form it has taken is the adoption of an historicist attitude which asserts that keeping old façades and hiding any new building behind them is better than anything totally new. The results are pitiful and border on the absurd. Old and new become caricatures, embodying the worst of both. "Façadism" represents a shallow, provincial view of history.

The present mood against new development has also inspired the most amazing and arbitrary "rules". For example, one can cite the objections of authorities in Melbourne, Australia to a large city building. They quote, verbatim, the recently proposed San Francisco plan and insist that this reactionary set of new rules, imported from halfway around the world, be adopted. This plan calls for the prohibition of buildings with flat roofs, of blank walls and for a "generous use of decorative embellishments". To demonstrate what benefits are offered to builders in return for compliance, these decorations are even allowed to protrude outside the zoning envelope! The San Francisco plan further requires buildings to be "shaped to appear delicate and of complex visual imagery". Worst of all, there is a dictate to "retain the street wall"; tall buildings are to have distinctive tops and shafts, that is, to construct "street-fronting bases" for all tall buildings.

Prevalent rules discourage limits to site coverage and, in fact, outlaw any towers which leave large portions of the ground level unbuilt. The irrationality of insisting that urban development be built to an index of fourteen to one, while at the same time having one hundred percent site coverage, is obvious. To allow an increase in the population on a city block to that extent and then to strangulate pedestrian circulation by restricting it to ten feet wide footpaths, is inhuman and unworkable. It is socially irresponsible to build to high indexes of twelve or fourteen unless there is a limit on site cover of no more than twenty-five to thirty-five percent. This should be so, not only for the sake of health and clarity of the inevitably huge structure that results, but also to generate some breathing space for the additional thousands of people who work in such buildings. In our increasingly crowded cities the aim should be to create as much genuinely useful open space (open to the sky or glass covered) on private land as possible, places of repose and recreation.

The fashion of solid street-fronting bases for towers is also highly questionable. One must reject it for practical and aesthetic reasons because it forces architects to design huge, deep, windowless, commercially-unviable podium spaces which are structurally and constructionally undesirable.

What lies behind all of this is nothing other than a misguided form of romanticism –an attempt to recreate eighteenth– and nineteenth– century urban patterns which evolved when population densities were much lower than today and when buildings were rarely more than three or four storeys high. By all means let there be enlightened, that is flexible, three-dimensional control strategies that protect the community from excesses: controls which make the intent understood and which can be amended with time. The design professions must, however, as a matter of principle, fight against governments being given the right to codify and thereby dictate design in detail. To allow such rules is absurd and contrary to fundamental freedom of action, freedom for the advancement and development of architecture. To stifle creativeness by law is intolerable. We should want no part of a system in which bureaucrats become powerful arbiters of taste, imposing a dictatorship over the language of form.

2. Opposition to Modern Architecture

Turning now from city planning to the subject of architectural theory and taste, and specifically to the issue of what architects choose to build, we find the reaction has been equally devastating. Much wordy journalism tells us that it is time to revert to the past and suggests that we go back to the 1920s and other fragmentary earlier sources in history for inspiration. Lumping together and labelling everything built in our time under the much maligned term "International Style", the media distort historical facts with great abandon.

To begin with, the term "International Style" is a misnomer. It was anathema to the methodology expounded by the pioneers of modern architecture. Walter Gropius himself expressed contempt for its use. To him the only structures which could truly be labelled "international" in style were "those classic colonnades, borrowed from the Greeks, placed in front of important buildings anywhere from Chicago to Moscow to Tokyo". For modern architecture, as conceived by its pioneers, was not a fixed set of forms but rather a way of thinking. It is an approach which "allows one to tackle a problem according to its peculiar conditions, not by ready-made dogma nor stylistic formula, but by an attitude towards the problems of our generation which is unbiased, original and elastic". Modern architecture could never be a style *per se*. It must remain in constant flux, responding not only to regional differences and social demands but also reflecting the changing visual language of art and the ever-expanding wealth of technological means. As the form-determining factors change, so too must the architectural expression.

In my own work this methodology has been simply a framework on which to hang very different and potentially changing images – the opposite to frozen stylistic moulds. It is an attitude towards design which can grow and mutate with the cultural essentials of time and place.

Unfortunately, however, the clarity of this concept and the specifics of its aesthetic components (built on the study of visual fundamentals) never became the guiding principle for building in our time. What had originally started as a fight against traditional "style" was utterly misunderstood and was imitated insensitively until it became so banal that it could itself be termed a style. Since the last war, unskilled, superficial images with hideous clichés have covered western cities and the understandable public distaste for these ubiquitous results finds its voice in the present day media war on the so-called "International Style". The attack is misdirected though. Journalists and opportunistic writers deliberately misrepresent facts, re-write history and cowardly discredit the dead pioneering initiators, blaming those whose work originated long-overdue movement away from the superficial "art for art's sake" architecture of the *fin de siècle* era.

Ironically, by Gropius' definition, those who today perpetrate and practise the "International Style" are none other than the "rats, posts and other pests" that Aldo van Eyck aptly referred to in his 1981 RIBA Annual Discourse. Who else but those he so lucidly describes would proceed from doing parodies of Le Corbusier to blending Albert Speer's Reichskanzlei with Mussolini's visions and dishing them up in Portland, Oregon – or suggest variations of the Mausoleum at Halicarnassos be put on top of Breuer's Whitney Museum in New York?

What is now proposed, seemingly unchallenged, is the very antithesis of the visual and technical concerns of our time. We are shown ponderous, earthbound, pyramidal compositions standing flatfootedly, exposing their childish broken pediment "metaphors" in order to make us feel closer to "history". Ignoring and defying all constructional, let alone structural, logic they are the tantrums of a rich, spoilt child delighting in being contrary and shocking us with corny stylistic idioms, not to say ludicrous bad taste.

The labels abound, supported by inept and obtuse verbiage: Adhocism, Pluralism, Contextualism, Post-Modernism, Inclusivism, Late-Modern, Post-Modern Classicism, etc... And the current schizophrenia oscillates in adulation between Post-Modernism and "Modernistic" Stylism (that painful fad of the 1930s) to the exhibitionistic display of technological acrobatics for its own sake. Rather than serving any constructional needs, the latter exposes the vulnerable arteries of a building to the elements, ensuring anything but the permanent life of the structure.

These, as any fashion, cloy the appetite. They are transient and self-extinguishing, grating and annoying the senses in the end. They are regressive, anti-intellectual modes -defying reason, art and technics. They are not a worthy product of our time, whose creed should be one of restraint and disdain for wilful waste or physical or visual extravagance.

The degeneration has indeed gone full circle. One need only remember the western architectural world's outrage at the cultural inferiority of communist East Berlin's Stalinallee, erected after the war at the same time Le Corbusier was building in Marseille. And now, in a complete reversal of roles, East Germany has rebuilt the Bauhaus structures better than new and Czechoslovakia has restored the Tugendhat House. They declared them national shrines while, in the west, Bofill builds a public housing scheme which boasts new classical orders made of precast concrete and gigantic fluted Roman columns for fire stairs. It is the kind of architecture that totalitarian regimes of both left and right have always favoured.

It could all be ignored if there were not the danger, due to all the wordy journalism surrounding and justifying it, of being taken literally by the young and uninitiated; of being blown up and catapulted into the significance of a new design philosophy.

A remark Marcel Breuer made to me in the 1950s puts these things in perspective. In discussion his reaction to the then fashionable classicism – that sugar-coated, misunderstood Miesian mode prevalent in America at that time – he said in German "Nur abwarten" (just wait patiently). And who remembers or takes this fad seriously now? Or who remembers the Brutalists in England with their pathetic imitations of Le Corbusier's rough concrete of the 1940s? With that record what lasting validity can be ascribed to the "metaphors" so verbosely elaborated to describe the present reversions to licentious decorative caprice?

3. Looking Forward

To me there is a discernible visual direction in our age. As manifested in our immediate history, the essence of this is best defined by the painter, Josef Albers: "Where the discrepancy between physical fact and psychic effect is maximised, there lies the threshold of art", and "One plus one is three – in art". This credo of getting the most aesthetically and physically for the least in effort and material is directly applicable to architecture. Not only is it valid for economic reasons, but it will heighten the value of that which, by a shortcut of the mind and with penetrating insight, finds Gordian Knot solutions to aesthetic, planning and constructional problems.

The simplistic way in which this essential element has been misinterpreted is the cause for much of the harm that has been done in the name of modern architecture. To do the minimal only leads to stagnation and rejection, but to do little in such a way that riches result, both visually and tangibly, that is where our direction lies.

From its earliest days the modern movement has emphasised the study of visual fundamentals of just how our eyes respond in predictable ways to visual phenomena. A study of these principles will make us realise how we see changes as other areas of our existence change. What was valid in 1930 can no longer be actively so today because our senses will respond differently to the altered social conditions and to advances in technology. Thus our notions of appropriate construction, of the way space should be ordered, of visual expression and the forms that derive from these concerns must, of necessity, be different from those of the past or of other cultural milieus.

For example, however much we may admire Le Corbusier's buildings, their twenty feet square span structures (which was all they could do economically then) are superseded today just as is their planning, plumbing and everything else about them. We may still find his spatial flow poetic, enticing and valid, though achieving it meant the use of excessive hand labour or constructional devices no longer realistically plausible.

We live in a world of vastly varying social and economic climates. I have built on four different continents and what is possible and in fact desirable in one country with ample, willing and undemanding labour but poor technology is unthinkable in a location with advanced industrial potential and high labour costs. Such considerations will inevitably produce regional differences in buildings even if the common aim is to create a subtle orchestration of spatial intricacies.

It is also evident that twentieth-century man's concept of space and how it should be organised has changed in a way which only our advancing technology can muster. Instead of the assemblies of connected finite volumes of the past, we now seek a sense of the infinite and yet simultaneously the intimate – a sense of the beyond in the immediacy of the present.

Likewise in the choice of the appropriate form our horizons broadened considerably with time. The initial puritanical rigidity has been allowed to widen into an all-encompassing search which even today is yielding a wealth of new expression. We have learned to borrow from the art forms of our time just as we have learned not to exclude history. By "history", of course, I do not mean the puerile adaption of decorative paraphernalia but rather a study of the essential forces behind the images of the past. For instance, the subtly brilliant geometric systems that came into being in the seventeenth and eighteenth centuries can inform our approach to developing system-oriented methods of construction. But the visual language must be new. I believe that visual tension, not the phlegmatic earthbound images of the past, speaks to our time; the channelling of space and surfaces in opposition, curve against countercurve, sun and shadow, the juxtaposition of compression to the surprise of release.

Even if the expression is exuberant or flamboyant, an economy of visual means will heighten the value of the result. Instead of creating an arbitrary assemblage of unrelated geometries, a single form element should be evolved and transformed, finding its echo throughout the work at every scale – a set of variations on a single visual theme.

Free rein must also be given to the expression of the laws of nature – not what is "imagined" to be so by many structurally naïve architects, but the unassailable physical truth of statics. Being born of the immutable and irrevocable truth of nature, the richness of expression which can result from such a search will have the irreplaceable quality of longevity, of remaining authentic as times change.

In our approach to constructional systems we architects generally have been far too simplistic, accepting any dull repetitiveness to be economically valid. Just as the revivalist architecture at the end of the last century was out of tune with the emerging industrial means, so I believe the design profession today is not responding adequately to either current technological and manpower conditions or new construction methodologies. That is why we are losing the grip on vital decision-making and are being replaced by hustling technicians. To design a tall building today, which simply takes too long to build, is a self-arresting process, a hollow victory realised only on paper.

It is our task to maximise systems of mechanisation appropriate to and "in tune" with the particular task. Even though these must vary in different socio-economic and industrial climates, one must not stop at the consideration of structure and covering only, as is so often the limit of prevalent thought. Rather, one must encompass simultaneously integral solutions to the problems posed by all the services required in a project, thereby avoiding the usual nightmarish afterthought complications of most modern buildings.

True modern architecture is not dead as some will have us believe. We have hardly started to explore the potential of its methodology. The high principles and clear moral consequentiality of the pioneers needs to be constantly interpreted anew. They demanded basic integrity and an intrinsic honesty of approach. Only by making these part of our work will the frontiers of development be pushed forward.

4. Finally

In dealing with the problems of our environment today it is not possible to ignore the much publicised, embarrassing notions expressed by, let us say, a less-than-erudite member of the Royal Family. Nor can one ignore certain self-appointed critics, even from the realm of academia, who speak and write in his defence. Nothing demonstrates more clearly the provincial and insensitive view of the visual arts in our time, than the insistent proposal to return to eighteenth- and nineteenth-century imagery – coupled with the claim that such a fossilised view of our culture is shared by the "masses".

The senses of the proposers have become so desperately stultified that they have assumed an aggressive stance in the media to defend their historically absurd and untenable position.

No-one would wish to condone the massive misdeeds perpetrated in much of the Anglo-Saxon world since World War II. England has consistently rejected and been generally immune to expressions of the visual language of our time. America showed promise for some decades (during the working presence of European pioneers) but finally only played at imitating superficial phenomena – ultimately showing its true cultural colours –reactionary provincialism. Unfortunately Australia is falling victim to the anti-modernist hysteria supported by the American architectural media.

Significantly, this debased reversion in Western culture is not shared in Scandinavian and other European countries that have a history of early developments in Modernism.

Near the end of our century it may be well for us to take heed of the almost one hundred year old inscription above the entrance to the Sezession Building in Vienna:

DER ZEIT IHRE KUNST

DER KUNST IHRE FREIHEIT

(To each era its art

To art its freedom)

One would think its simple wisdom should not need to be stated again.

Biographical Notes

Professor Nathan Glazer
Professor of Education and Sociology,
Harvard University

Sallyanne Atkinson
Lord Mayor of Brisbane 1985-91

Professor Roger Scruton
Professor of Aesthetics, Birkbeck College,
University of London

Mr Richard MacCormac
Architect, MacCormac, Jamieson and Prichard, London

Professor Norman Hammond
Professor of Archaeology,
Boston University

Professor Dell Upton
Professor of Architecture,
University of California, Berkeley

Mr Daryl Jackson
Architect, Daryl Jackson Pty Ltd., Melbourne

Mr Hans Hallen
Architect, Godfrey Spowers and Hallen, Sydney

Mr Harry Seidler A.C. O.B.E
Architect, Harry Seidler & Associates, Sydney

The Boston, Melbourne, Oxford Conversazioni on Culture and Society
Executive Committee
Dr John Silber, *President,* Boston University
The Hon. Mr Justice R.F. McGarvie, *Chancellor,* La Trobe University
Professor Claudio Véliz, *Director,* The University Professors, Boston University
Sir Claus Moser K.C.B, C.B.E., F.B.A., *Warden,* Wadham College, Oxford

Acknowledgments

The Boston, Melbourne, Oxford Conversazioni on Culture and Society gratefully acknowledges the generous grants and assistance given by the Brazier Ella & Mitchell Fund and Harry Bunting Estate (administered by ANZ Executors & Trustee Company Limited), Boston University, CRA Limited, the E.B. Myer Charity Fund (administered by Perpetual Trustees Victoria Limited), Godfrey & Spowers Australia Pty. Ltd., La Trobe University, The Pratt Group, The Shell Company of Australia Limited and the Victorian Ministry for the Arts, whose encouraging and imaginative support has made it possible to convene this conversazione. Acknowledgement is due to the Curtis Brown Group Ltd on behalf of the Estate of Lawrence Durrell. Elizabeth Robertson kindly prepared the type script for this publication.

In The Boston, Melbourne, Oxford Conversazioni on Culture and Society, each of the three participating universities sponsors an international conversazione once every three years. On the occasion of its sesquicentennial celebration in 1989, Boston University inaugurated the series with "A Metaphor for our Times". It was then Melbourne's turn, and in July 1990 La Trobe University sponsored a conversazione "On The Public Face of Architecture". In September 1991 Wadham College, Oxford, hosted the third one on "Schools and Society"; and in October 1992 the fourth conversazione will take place in Boston to consider "The Worth of Nations".

The Boston, Melbourne, Oxford Conversazioni on Culture and Society.
The Melbourne Committee, 1991-1993.

Mr Tim Acton
Mr Anthony Adair
Professor John Anderson
Professor Geoffrey Blainey
Mr Peter Chew
Mrs Eril Deighton
The Hon. James Guest M.L.C.
Sir Rupert Hamer K.C.M.G.
Mrs Jill Kitson
Emeritus Professor Dame Leonie Kramer, D.B.E.
Mr John E. Lewis
Mr Sam Lipski
Mr George Littlewood
Mr Ranald Macdonald
The Hon. Mr Justice R.E. McGarvie, Chairman
Emeritus Professor Michael Osborne
Most Reverend Bishop George Pell
Miss Dorothy Pizzey
Dr Roger Sworder
Professor Claudio Véliz
Professor The Hon. Evan Walker M.L.C.